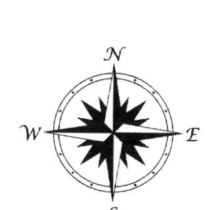

SHORT
SWEET
&
SACRED

59 COURAGEOUS STORIES
FROM LIFE COACHES WHO DARED TO CHANGE THE DIRECTION OF THEIR LIVES

VOLUME III

Published by Elevate Publishing, Roswell, Georgia

ISBN 978-0-9991949-9-7 (paperback)

Printed in the United States of America

A big thank you to Cliff Pelloni at Elevate Publishing,
and for your team who supported us through the process
of creating and printing this beautiful book.

A heartfelt shout out to Colton Weidner at Done
For You Technology, and how you have provided the
lovely websites for the authors of this book.

And to each and every coach, thank you for being such a loving group
of women and men. It's honorable how you are actively devoting
your lives to helping people—your stories are transformational.

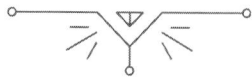

Contents

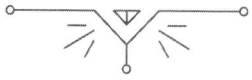

Introduction

Many of us have heard the saying, "Humans are creatures of habit." We tend to drive the same way to work, go through the same morning routine, end up in the same kinds of relationships, and everything in between. My thought is, if we are creatures of habit, why not change our habits to change our lives? This is exactly what the 59 Life Coaches showcase in this book.

Each storyteller shares their true and personal journey of changing the direction of their life for the sake of a breakthrough. They are inspiring! These are true stories from around the world that highlight hope that can become our own. After all, you have access to the same power to change your life!

As you read these beautiful stories of wisdom, I will invite you to open your heart to the possibility that anything is possible! What is possible for someone, is possible for everyone.

—Erin Davenport

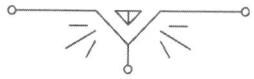

Piece of Cake!

Mariana Nadina Simon
ARGENTINA

It's a wonderful afternoon and I'm enjoying a colorful spring on Saturday. Mmmmmhhhh!!!

I love to hear the tiny tuneful birds as I look at this lake with these huge green trees and inhale their fresh sweet smell. And I'm breathing. Yes, I'm breathing in a calm atmosphere.

The best part is the setting sun after an intense three-hour sports session. My eyes, my brain, my body, and my heart are feeling relaxed and joyful.

After an exhausting training session and my brief contemplative state, I also realize I am smelling like a dirty, sweaty pig, and I am thirsty and cramping. And I am starving! It's time to visit the shower.

After my shower comes the best part—teatime! Yay! I'm happy to be with two of my teammates, and we find a seat at the coffee shop to order our teas and cakes. We are relaxing and soaking in the beautiful lake with its birds, trees, and fragrances.

We are chatting excitedly and then I start to perceive a shift in the moods of my friends, and I can see it in their gazes. They seem to be stressed, but I don't understand why. It's almost as if a black cloud has settled on their heads.

And then, with a whispering voice, one of them explains to me, "I don't want to sit at this table because the waiter is an angry, horrible, dumb man." Simultaneously, my other friend chimes in, "Yes! Last week this oldie was being nasty. I felt so uncomfortable."

"What? No way! Look at him! He looks like an old man trying to earn an additional income . . . for sure he would prefer to stay home and rest instead of waiting tables." They start to gossip and they answer me in a mocking tone. "We are going to sit for a while at this empty table, but because there is no other available. As soon as another one is released, we are changing tables so that a different waiter can serve us. We know you usually have a positive vibe, but we assure you that this time you will not succeed with your charm and enchantment. But well . . . maybe we can challenge you to change his mood and for you to have a friendly interaction with him in less than five minutes, but we warn you that you will fail!"

The game is on my field. I have no doubts. Internally, I'm sure it's a vibration issue. I know I must trust my instincts and I don't let myself be influenced by their bad vibes. But simultaneously, I'm feeling that a heavy energy has begun to enter my body.

Stop . . . Breathe . . . Repeat this process. After ten seconds, an amused answer slips from my mouth. "Challenge accepted! Watch me!" With a huge smile and an endearing look, I call the waiter. He approaches me with a serious face and asks me what I want to drink. And, right there, I raise the bet and ask him for help: "I'm starving! What would you recommend from the menu? I don't know what to choose!"

Surprisingly, he answers me with, "I have a huge list of options to recommend to you! Let me sit at your table and I'll tell you what we have, to see what you are tempted with!" He pulls the chair to the side, sits down, and begins to tell me about the more than 20 varieties of cakes they bake at the restaurant.

"But now I'm more confused than before! I love everything you've recommended! What would *you* eat?" And then, with him feeling like the best adviser and waiter in Argentina, he tells me, "I'm going to help you a little more. I'm going to bring you a slice of each cake and you decide what to choose. Let your eyes decide." He gets up and goes to the kitchen to find and bring all of the cakes.

Two minutes later, I let myself be guided by the waiter, I decide what to eat, and I ask him why he works here. He tells me, "I retired a couple of years ago, and at home I get bored. I prefer to do something and put myself in the service of people." Feeling more connected, we start telling jokes and laughing.

After that, he asks my friends what they want and they make their requests. The waiter disappears into the kitchen. I turn around to look at the faces of my two friends. They are stunned— looking at me with wide eyes and unable to speak.

Right there I tell them my secret. "The only difference between you and me is that I know how to use my energy. And I won the bet! You are paying the bill today!"

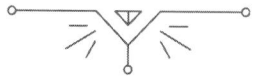

Finding Me

Lisa Phelan
NEW HAMPSHIRE, USA

It is a chilly fall day. I am sitting on a well-used couch with a blanket around me. The room is small and filled with books, crystals, and candles, and at my feet, a very large Golden Retriever named Honey Bear. This room is very familiar to me; I have been coming here every Tuesday for the last year. On this particular Tuesday, the emotional weight of depression and darkness is heavy and even the warmth and light from the sun streaming through the window cannot change how I feel.

"Lisa . . . did you hear me?" The voice is coming from the chair across from me. I turn to look at the woman sitting there. She is a remarkable woman, my life-line for the past year. Nedra is an unconventional therapist. I have been to other therapists where I talk, they listen, and fifty minutes later I am out the door. There is no time limit here. She listens and asks questions for as long as I need. She is direct.

One of our first times together, she gave me a piece of advice. She made a circle with her hands and said, "This is my plate." She made a circle towards me and said, "This is your plate. I have s**t on my plate and you have s**t on your plate. Don't put your s**t on my plate and don't allow people to put their s**t on your plate." At first, I was caught off guard by the profanity coming from a professional, but it's this directness that made me know she was different and I was in the right place . . . finally.

I am thirty-six years old, married, with two beautiful children, a girl age 10 and a boy age 7. I live in an upscale community in an amazing new home. I have a new job making six figures. We drive expensive cars. We ski every weekend. I coach my kids in soccer, volunteer at school, and host dinner parties. People ask me, "How do you do it all?" My life looks picture perfect.

The truth is, I am broken inside. I absolutely hate my job. I am working in sales in the high tech industry. Sales is the last thing I ever wanted to do with my life. In 1989, when I was graduating from college, there were not a lot of jobs and the only job I was offered was in sales. Begrudgingly, I took it. I felt pressure from my fiancé to get a "real job."

Every morning, I woke up and asked myself, "Should I take a left or right today?" Inevitably, I would end up at the local coffee shop giving myself a pep talk to go knock on doors. When I first took the job, I thought I would do this for a year and then find a job I love. Unfortunately, I started making lots of money and the more I made, the more we bought . . . bigger house, better cars, vacations.

Before I knew it, I was stuck. My new sales job put my earnings at a whole different level and the pressure to perform was high. We moved a year ago to a new town; home prices were twice as expensive, and to get a comparable house, which my husband wanted, our mortgage payment would double. I took the new job to make him happy. I left every morning with a knot in my stomach. I came home tired and drained, with very little energy to make dinner or help my kids with schoolwork. I had little patience on many days and would yell at them.

When I finally got them to bed I felt so bad about myself, for yelling and not really being present for them. I started beating myself up about what a bad mother I had become. The wine started flowing, shutting off my brain so I didn't have to think about how truly unhappy, broken, and alone I felt.

This brings me to my marriage Five days before our wedding, I tried to call it off. I sat down with him and told him I couldn't do it. His response was, "If you don't go through with it, you will embarrass me in front of my family and friends." When I continued, he said, "How will your mom feel about losing $5,000?" Like a good girl, I went through with it even though I tried one more last-ditch effort. I asked my maid of honor and bridesmaids to take the limo into Boston and go dancing instead. No one was willing to go into the church to tell him, so down the aisle I went.

As I walked down the aisle, my 24-year-old self said, "Lisa, hold your head high, your shoulders back, you can always get a divorce." This is how I went into my marriage and this was a frequent thought throughout the marriage.

Again I hear my name, "Lisa, are you okay?" Tears stream down my face as I look over at her. She asks me a crucial and life-changing question—a question for which I have no answer. "What do *you* love and need?" I stare at her blankly. I didn't know what she was asking me. "Lisa, you know what everyone else loves. You know what your kids love and need, your husband, your boss, your friends; what do you love and need?"

I don't have an answer for her. I have been sucked into the quicksand of life, trying to keep myself from sinking. I met my husband when I was nineteen, and life just seemed to happen. I never had a chance to really discover what and who I want to be.

This question, "What do I love and need?" would take me on a beautiful, yet sometimes rocky, journey into self-discovery and decision. I quit my job, ended my marriage lovingly, found the love of my life, and discovered my passion for helping people find out who they are and what they love. I make decisions that honor the beautiful soul inside of me. I design my own life, speak my truth, listen to my still small voice, and trust in God. After years of searching, I have finally found me.

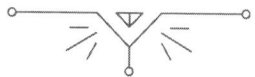

Secrets of the Between

Shana Horrigan
WEST VIRGINIA, USA

Mesmerized by the falling leaves dancing in the wind, I sit on my porch. One, two, three, pause, two, three, repeat. The drip, drip, drip of raindrops falling from the clogged gutter are beating a waltz on the deck.

Winter is just around the corner. I shudder with the imagined cold.

My mind travels down memory lane to a snowy clearing deep in the woods. Fragrant pine boughs bend deep from the weight of fresh snow. Someone mounted candles on their tips. They cast a magic glow on the hollowed cradle of a fallen tree. I inhale the frigid air and taste its iciness. My breath rises visibly as it warms the mouthpiece of my trumpet. Another inhale and the brilliant, almost heartbreaking sound of "Silent Night" pierces the calm to fill this space out of time.

I'm startled from my reverie by an obnoxious ringtone reminder. Operant conditioning, I think, as I jump up and abandon the beautiful otherworldliness, with its reverence, peace and quiet. Instead of salivating like a dog for food, overwhelm and anxiety flood my system. There is nothing that I would love more just about now than that peace and quiet from my childhood. Instead, I turn back to my laptop to type.

Tick tock says the clock.

One more minute, says I.

Tick tock, the offending time piece insists.

I know, I know, the essay is due.

Not only is the deadline for the essay ringing shrilly from my phone, but every molecule in my environment demands my attention—people, pets, household, work—in an unending cacophony. Resigned, my tired body holds up a sign: Life support systems dropping by the minute, the minute . . . tick tock!

I jolt awake as my head hits the desk. With every passing birthday, I feel time compress. There is more to do and less time to do it, more competing interests clamoring for attention, welcome and unwelcome. More data to process, more useless information to filter. More demands and fewer rewards. I survive by escaping into the liminal space of daydream's endless possibilities.

I am chronically exhausted. Lacking quality sleep from sleep apnea does not help, I am told. And so, I get a CPAP—yay, me. I look like an elephant and sound like a drowning walrus as I gasp, "I love you, good night"—this is such a turn-on in bed. I thank the stars for a loving and understanding partner with a quirky sense of humor. But it is not the panacea for which I was hoping. I seek more professional help.

Even between a fractured skull as a young child, severe misdiagnosed symptoms in puberty, and lifelong labels like "daydreamer" and "space cadet," the ADHD diagnosis still comes as a surprise. So much of my life makes sense now, and I feel relieved.

Commanding my brain to "just do it" is an exercise in futility. If

I could "just do it" I would have just done it. Focusing on anything is almost impossible when your brain behaves like an unruly puppy while someone shouts "squirrel" every five minutes. Everything is equally important, or at least has the potential to be. Getting "lost" in a department store for hours is just par for the course.

With proper treatment for my crippling anxiety and depression, dysfunctional coping starts to melt away. I feel like myself again for the first time in forty years. What doesn't melt away is four decades of accumulated clutter and chaos from attempting to bootstrap my brain's executive functions.

Living without efficient and effective systems, organization, habits, and routines is exhausting. The twenty-plus books on organization in my bookcase and other copious aborted attempts at creating order are a testament to my resilience, determination, and desperation. I even tried to color code my kitchen once. Who does that?!

As I am learning organizational skills and building effective systems, I am creating space, physically, mentally, and emotionally. Automating repetitive tasks is opening up my time and energy. I have more capacity now to decide what is important. How unimportant most things really are is astounding.

I am releasing what I clung to because I was afraid to lose something potentially vital—especially memories. Mom's worthless stamp collection—gone. VHS tapes along with them—bye. An industrial-size supply of inherited office supplies, kept just in case I might need to supply an industry, is I hope now supplying an industry. It is a slow and intentional process.

Each layer of clutter is fraught with emotion. Grief traps abound. Sadness, anger, and regret lay in wait and skitter out like noxious spiders. Wistful memories, warm thoughts and mischievous giggles emerge. I let them wash over me. I hold on to none of them.

Slowly, as I gain room to breathe, I learn to savor the in-between. The empty space on the shelf. The blank page in the calendar. I am arresting time. Holding space. That moment between inhale and exhale when life itself seems suspended. A house in a drawing defined by the space around it. Like negative space in art, the rests in music are a shift in perspective. Sound and silence as one. Doing and non-doing, action and stillness, the dance of my life.

Drip, pause, drip, drip. The raindrops are hitting the deck more infrequently now. The wind has died down, leaving the deck covered in leaves. The gutter is still clogged with debris. But at least there is a chance it will be cleaned out this year, leaving it empty, ready to receive the first snow. And this is something to celebrate.

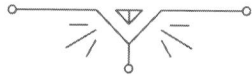

90 Years, or
One Year 90 Times?

Joan M. Luke
CALIFORNIA, USA

The white sheets are too cozy to abandon. "Stay in bed," I hear my thoughts whisper. A decade of carpool schedules is over, and no brown bag lunches beckon to be made. My board member appointment terms are complete, there are no colleges to visit, and our four children are educated and gone.

I am part of the "quiet quitters" workforce. My once-thriving home-based business, full of purpose, financial success, peer support, and joy is dwindling, frustrating and stale. I do as little as possible and hope no one notices, including me. I cringe as I see 3500+ unread emails. I skip the emails and spend the next hours scrolling through social media apps in bed, depressed.

My suitcase is open on the floor, waiting for me to pack. Annual ski vacations, tropical beach getaways, Wine Festival in the mountains, VIP golf tournaments, and girls' shopping weekends fill the calendar, and it feels repetitive. I live a dream life. So why am I still in bed, waiting for the urge to get up?

"Where did it go? Where did my purpose, joy, excitement, clarity, and connectedness to God go?" I feel numb.

Ping! The text alert sounds. It is an invitation from my best friend. I quickly glance only at the date and time and respond, yes, from a place of desperation, pain, and hope.

And what is up with her? The launch of a new chapter in her life has her on fire! She is dating the love of her life, sitting on multiple boards of directors, living and working in Europe every summer, and now she is speaking and writing. She is electrifying to be around, and I am in awe of her transformation.

The invitation day is here. I sit in the front row of her workshop and take pictures to support and cheer her on with enthusiasm and wonder. Halfway through her presentation, she states with conviction, "You can live 90 years, or you can live one year 90 times." I repeat it to myself as the idea sinks deep into my Soul. The realization hits me hard! I am living the same good life year after year. I should be grateful I live a blessed life. Like many others, I am taught to be thankful and not want more. I am stuck, and it feels awful.

Listening further, my friend invites me to look at two sacred signals to create a new dynamic chapter. "Make a list of your longings and discontents," she instructs. I feverishly make my list: I long to respect myself more, have a clear purpose, jump out of bed with joy, and be grateful for my robust health and a calendar that excites me with new challenges, new people, and new places. And most importantly, I yearn to be more connected and dependent on God and His infinite resources to create the seemingly impossible.

I crave a deeper connection with my husband, with fun and new shared activities. I long to write a bestselling book I have been drafting for fifteen years. I am discontented with the amount of my financial contribution to our household and philanthropic donations. And then I ponder, "What regrets will I have when I die?"

This "long" list exposes the hole in my Spirit. The next instruction is to write a three-year vision on "What would I love?" I feel the energy inside me shift. This list is a sacred gift to create my next dream. My Soul's desire is to serve others joyfully with my God-given gifts and talents. I am 56 years old and declare, "I am not too old and will never be too old to pursue my dreams." Nervous and excited, I sign up for 90 days of coaching, support, and curriculum. This step forward is full of excitement, hope, and anticipation for more.

My newly-learned thinking, decisions, and actions bring new results. The alarm sounds, and I wake up with energy, excitement, and clarity, throwing off the white sheets and leaping out of bed. My program of weekly coaching calls and support brings new awakenings, vocabulary, and "innerstanding." Each week, I commit to the action step I can take with what I have and from where I am—moving in the direction of my three-year vision. My calendar now boasts weekly dance lessons under the stars with my husband whispering, "One, two, three, four," and me giggling. Three mornings a week, at sunrise, I put my toes in the sand, living a long-time dream of playing beach volleyball with other athletes. And my book is written and is now being edited.

As I check off the dreams I've achieved, I ask, "What else would I love? What is my next great mission?" What would make this day, this month, and this year extraordinary? I hear a still voice whisper, "Be a coach. Coaching is your sacred life work and mission." *Yes!* This clarity, knowingness with innerstanding, illustrates my divine connection to God. "Yes! I would love to speak on stages, teach powerful truths, coach to support dreams, and celebrate others as they design a life they love." I take a step and invest in myself for the maximum degree of this program and study a rigorous curriculum. I then certify for coaching at the highest level of this Spirit-based, renowned program. I am living my beautiful dream!

Regenerated and transformed, I now rise each day at 5 AM. I design my day with a powerful morning ritual and a cup of espresso. I delight in reviewing a calendar of my client Zoom calls, upcoming speaking engagements across the country, scheduled webinars, and my study of the art and science of this great work. My speaking and coaching business is thriving and contributing double, almost triple, my previous income. Helping clients connect to the power within them—transmuting their good lives into full-spectrum extraordinary lives, elevates their inner joy and self-respect, and mine too.

My suitcase sits on the floor; this time, I am packing for a new, never-before-experienced adventure. Plans to visit the African villages we donate to monthly are on the itinerary. I am grateful I am living my Soul's purpose in serving others and transforming the world. This is *one year like no other!* "And what will the next year bring?" I ask. One thing I know, the year will be extraordinary and designed and lived like no other year. No regrets. I love my life!

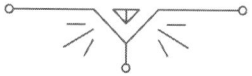

A Life Transformed

Donusia L. Lipinski
SOUTH CAROLINA, USA

I am driving back to Evergreen, wondering why my 16-year-old son, Collin, never showed up for our meeting in Denver. I call several times and leave messages. No answer.

It's January 12th, 2004, around 7 PM. I approach my intersection to get home, but it is blocked. There are red and blue flashing lights, police cars, an ambulance, and a big SUV facing the wrong direction.

As I drive past the intersection, I glance back to see if another vehicle is involved. For a split second, my heart skips a beat. I see the back end of a little red car that looks like Collin's. My eyes must be playing tricks on me, I tell myself. Then I look again, and this time, somehow, I see the unmistakable back end of Collin's little red car.

My heart starts beating faster. I cannot think straight. I am trying to convince myself that it is not Collin's little red car, praying, "Please, God, please don't let that be him." I am begging, "God, please. Please let him be okay."

As I turn down the frontage road, I see Collin's friends crying as they hold each other. A mom approaches me and puts her arms around me. She confirms that Collin was headed toward Denver when the SUV turned in front of him. Collin swerved to avoid her, but unfortunately, the front end of her SUV hit him broadside.

I see Collin's car; the top is cut off. I start running to the car and they turn me back. "But that's my son in there!" They do not let me in. I feel helpless. I am desperate to know where Collin is and if he is okay.

It feels like an eternity before my worst nightmare is confirmed. Collin is dead. Time stands still. I cannot fathom that my baby Collin died in a car accident less than a mile from home. I am bereft. I do not know what to do with the pain of loss.

During these hours, days, and months, I struggle to make sense of it all, asking "why?" questions for which there are no answers. My world does not feel safe anymore, and I do not know where to turn. I am drinking too much. I am isolated. I was always the strong one, or at least that is what I fashioned myself to be. Who would want to be around me if I am sad? If I cry? If I am vulnerable?

In the aftermath of the accident, Collin's friends and I create a tight bond. They give me a window into Collin's spirit and the bright light he was for them. I give them a safe refuge to remember, to cry, to laugh, to share with each other and with me his ability to make others laugh, to brighten up a room with his smile, how fiercely loyal he was: a peacemaker, inclusive, creative, and so loved. I feel so blessed by this community, and I know we are helping each other cope with our loss.

I am at a crossroads in my life, and I feel spent. Collin's death was preceded by the dissolution of my marriage five months earlier, followed by my dad's passing six weeks to the day of Collin's death. In addition, the trial of the woman whose SUV killed Collin is coming up. I am empty. There is too much trauma and drama, and I am afraid I could subject myself to a malpractice suit if I continue my work as an immigration lawyer. I decide to close my law office.

Collin's death is a wake-up call. I recognize I am on a collision course with fate, drinking to escape my problems, working long hours, and feeling like I am carrying the world's weight on my shoulders. I am being driven by pain and am blaming circumstances outside of myself for all that is happening.

I know there must be more to life than what I am experiencing, some reason for the circumstances of my life. I begin to question the meaning of my life and why I am here—wanting to know Collin's purpose and why he died so young.

I wake up to the reality that the only way to heal and find answers to my questions about the meaning of life and my purpose is to go deeper spiritually. Opening myself to the journey of healing and recovery is one of the greatest gifts I have received through Collin's death. Though the journey is not always easy, the rewards of self-discovery are priceless.

As a result of Collin's death, I am learning to live in the present moment and not as a victim of my circumstances and conditions. I know there is a choice about how I respond to life. Do I choose love or hate? Do I choose to be compassionate or indifferent? Do I choose humility or arrogance?

The spiritual journey emerging from Collin's death enables me to forgive the woman who drove the SUV and to forgive myself for the guilt and shame I have felt for so many years. I am more joyful, free, and open as a result.

Collin's death is a reminder that I live in a Universe where there are infinite possibilities. We are all connected by and through love, and within me, within all of us, there is a power greater than any circumstance, situation, or condition.

I did not predict that I would learn to live and connect with my heart and purpose through Collin's death. I did not realize that his death would stretch me, take me deeper, challenge me, and cause me to grow in ways I could never have imagined.

Collin also left one last gift for me. After his death, we found a large piece of construction paper in his bedroom, freely overflowing with thirty-two "wisdom quotes" by mentors such as Einstein, Thoreau, Aristotle, and others. The following quote, written boldly with a black magic marker, speaks to my heart.

Death is more universal than life: everyone dies, but not everyone lives. This quote captures Collin's spirit. He lived his life fully and wholeheartedly. It is his legacy.

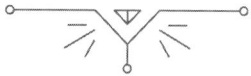

Everything Always Works Out

Julie Carlisle
UTAH, USA

"Why is this happening to us?" "Life is so cruel!" "Why are we being punished?"

My husband just gave his employers his two-week notice because we are finally starting our new Wood Fired Oven pizza restaurant. We have had so much fun finding the location and getting everything ready to go. We have the lease papers in hand for the building and are waiting for the lenders to send the closing papers over to be signed. This loan will enable us to begin some needed renovations to the building in order to open our restaurant.

Our lender calls to inform us that they need a lot of new information before they can give us our loan. Our loan officer is just as surprised as we are since the loan is secured and we are only waiting to sign the closing papers—or so we think. We do as they ask and give them what they need.

Another phone call comes much later and we are informed that the institution is being frozen and unable to service any loans at this time. This is the day that our lender, the fourth largest bank holding company in the US, tanks, and it's the beginning of the great recession of 2008. It is the most severe recession since the Great Depression of the 1930s.

I can't believe it! Now what are we going to do? There is no back-up plan, and my husband can't go back to his job. I begin to spiral down into a pit of despair and fear, full of panic and anxiety. I know I have to pull myself together and find solutions. We have six young children to clothe and feed.

Our first move is putting the house up for sale—we won't be able to pay the mortgage on it now. The real estate agent is a friend who lives nearby. He shares, "I'm happy to list it, but the market is stagnant and the reality of selling a big home like yours is very unlikely." We don't have a choice, so we list it.

A few months go by and no realtor has shown the house, even once. And what's worse is our savings are dwindling and we cannot pay this mortgage any longer. My husband and I do not even consider foreclosure an option, so we put our heads together to come up with a solution.

We decide we will offer a lease-option on the house and we let our real estate agent know this. He loves the idea and tells us that he and his wife have been looking for a bigger home, and this may be a good option for them. As we leave our beautiful home the week before Christmas, we are devastated, and our hearts are heavy with the knowledge that there will be no "Christmas" for the kids this year.

The day before we leave, we find a box left on our doorstep with all the fixings for a turkey dinner and a gift for each of us. How thoughtful of our neighbors! We can now leave with an attitude of gratitude for such wonderful friends and neighbors. This delicious meal and these gifts provide nourishment in many meaningful ways.

Our family starts our three-hour journey to a home my husband's sister owns. She lets us know we can stay as long as we need to. Since we won't have any gifts to give to the kids on Christmas, my husband comes up with a great idea. We can spend it giving our time and serving someone else. We will find a way or a place to serve others for Christmas this year.

This makes an otherwise depressing Christmas much more inviting. The kids seem really excited about it too. During our drive, I call local soup kitchens and food pantries to volunteer. "We're sorry, but some of your kids are too young to volunteer," they say. I reassure myself that it's okay. I know we will find something we can all do together.

We finally pull up to the house that we will be living in while we make an unintended new beginning. When we open the door, we are all surprised to see a fully decorated Christmas tree with the lights on! Underneath the tree, there are wrapped Christmas presents for everyone.

My husband's brother comes by the next day with his two little ones. He's going through a divorce. "Can we join you for the holidays?" he asks. We are so happy and grateful, because now we can serve someone, as we intended to do all along! With gratitude in our hearts, we share the turkey dinner and the gifts provided by others, and we enjoy our time spent together as family. It is a true celebration of love and service!

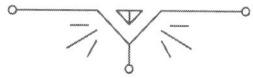

Into Flight

Benjamin B. Blackett

RHODE ISLAND, USA

It's a Tuesday afternoon during early September in the small countryside town of Les Vans in the South of France. At the feet of the Ardèche mountains, I am sitting in the grass under a large shady tree on the south side of the field they call "l'atterrissage"—meaning the "landing field"—for paragliders.

I am waiting for my turn to take a ride up the mountain with my co-pilot to take my first paragliding flight ever. I am 56, and this is a dream I've had for a long time. Until today, I have mostly thought, "Well, maybe someday I'll do it," but with a larger part of me believing, "Maybe I never will." But I think back to about ten months ago.

My mentor makes an invitation, "Let's commit to doing one of our bucket list activities within the year." To a room full of people I declare, "I will paraglide before we reunite as a group in a year."

As soon as I make the commitment, terror shoots through me. I laugh to myself aloud, "Yeah right, how is that possibly going to happen?" I can't even talk about it with another soul . . . mostly because I am certain if I talk about it, I may talk myself out of it.

The day before I leave for France, I tell one person I know that I have this on my mind. "I want to tell you just in case something goes wrong . . . and I am still not certain I will do it." The fear seems to grow.

Arriving in France, a part of me knows it's now or . . . possibly never. So, I make a call to École de Parapente, a paragliding school, and make a reservation.

Driving to the field is a challenge. The hotel I am staying at is an hour's drive away. I get in the car and start driving. I find I am hyperventilating every five minutes.

"Just breathe!" I instruct myself out loud. "Deep breaths."

After 45 minutes of driving, I start talking myself off the ledge . . .

"Don't turn around!"

"You will be fine!"

"They are waiting for you!"

"You have already given them your credit card number!"

"You'll be fine!"

"Just keep driving!"

"And keep breathing!"

I arrive at what I assume is the correct address, and there is no one there. I call and find out I'm in the wrong place. "Backtrack and come to . . ." they tell me. I follow their directions the best I can, but I know I haven't found where I am supposed to be. I call again. "Hold on right where you are! I am sending someone to come and get you." He finds me and brings me to l'atterissage.

Coming back from my thoughts and to the present moment,

I am on the side of the field and continuing to watch other paragliders land . . . one after another, after another, after another . . .

Oh, that doesn't look too hard . . . perhaps I can do that. And I am also watching other paragliders taking off from the top of the mountain in the distance . . . *can I do that?*

Suddenly the call comes, "Tout le monde dans la voiture!"

Eight of us pile into an Isuzu jeep with a large rack on top containing parachutes. We start the journey up the mountain on a slim road that allows only one vehicle at a time. I speak French well, but my mother tongue is English. I am barely aware of the conversation around me. I am too shocked by the fact that I am on my way to jumping off the side of a mountain. I don't even know who my pilot is.

Three quarters of the way up the mountain, I introduce myself to the man sitting next to me to help clear my mind of my fears. He turns out to be my pilot, and he is not very talkative—which increases my fear.

We arrive at the top. On the right side of us there is a straight drop down. On our left I see the runway, which is a short field of grass that is perhaps 25 meters long and at a descending 45-degree angle before it leads to a straight drop-off.

My co-pilot lays our parachutes on the ground, gives me a harness to climb into, clips himself to the parachute and me in my harness to him. We are ready to go.

He goes over the instructions, I wait for him to direct me, and then I do *exactly* as he says. On his command, we take three steps forward and stop . . . so the parachute lifts off the ground behind us and fills with air. On his command again, we run forward as fast as we can, leaning downhill. He tells me that we will continue running even once our feet are off the ground and until he tells me to stop. No hesitation, no pausing, no leaning back, and no sitting down. I tell him I understand.

Before take-off he then says, "D'accord, maintenant nous attendons!"

What? We have to wait?

"Why?"

"Because there might not be enough wind and we might be too heavy!"

What?

So, we wait . . . and wait . . . and wait for twelve and a half minutes. It feels like an eternity.

Suddenly he says, "Allez, avancez!"

I take three steps.

"Arrêtez!"

I stop.

We pause for about three seconds, then again "Allez, avancez!"

And we start running again . . .

Then, as if by magic, after only perhaps three more steps, our feet are off the ground, and we are airborne. A few more strides and my pilot tells me I can stop running and sit back into the seat of the harness.

It is magic! It is miraculous, and it is absolutely stunning. One of the most beautiful moments of my life is unfolding. There is the sun, the sky, and no sound of wind because we are riding the wind . . . complete silence . . . and the mountain top falls away behind us.

My pilot is very generous. He is answering all kinds of questions about how it works, how the wind works, and what it takes to become a pilot. He circles us around so our chute rises up higher and higher until we are actually above the mountain top, we just lifted off from. I can see down both sides of the mountain, and all the way to Avignon—which is about 100 kilometers away.

This is freedom! This is bliss! There is no more room for fear amidst the magic. We land safely and effortlessly. My vision expands again, and my new bucket list item is born—a solo flight.

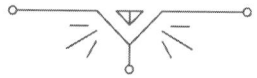

Changing Focus

Renee Leigh Crane
TEXAS, USA

My heart is breaking. Tears well in my eyes and spill down my cheeks. The road in front of me is becoming blurry, so I pull off the road to safety. I cry tears of frustration, knowing that it will be months before I see them again.

I've just left my daughter's home, where I have been for a week. She gave birth to a second daughter, and I have been in total grandma mode taking care of their oldest daughter, who is just 18 months old. I have two adorable granddaughters now, and I want to be a part of their lives, but I live 1,200 miles away and work full-time. How can I visit more often? I only have so much vacation time, and travel can be expensive.

At the same time, my son and his military family have recently moved and are only 700 miles away from me. On the bright side, his home is at a good overnight stopping point on the way to my daughter's. His two children are now in school full-time, and I want to be in their lives more too. If only there was a way to figure out how to get more vacation time. Then, I could spend time with his family, go to my daughter's, and see my grandkids again on the way back. Sounds like a win-win!

Back at home, my heart aches every day. I begin to look for jobs closer to them so I can still work and see them often. I apply to a few jobs, but nothing feels like the right answer. One day, I discover that the company I work for has a facility a few hours from both of their houses!

I find myself frequently checking the job postings for this facility—I am hoping that I can transfer there. All the while, my desire to get closer only gets more persistent by the day. In frustration, I tell myself that this is probably a pipedream that won't work out. The burning desire I once had becomes a small, smoldering flame.

Time passes by and I spontaneously decide to check the job postings at this other facility—just in case something popped up. It's been a few months since I last looked.

Oh my gosh . . . they have a posting! And it is the *exact* job I have at my current location. That burning desire builds again, and my heart is swelling with possibilities. I am so excited that I call my daughter and tell her there may be a way for me to get closer after all.

I apply for the job immediately. Soon after, I have an interview and a couple of discussions with the production manager. I feel good about this, I mean, I know the company, and I know the job. My current boss has given me a glowing review—I believe the odds are in my favor.

It's a Friday in October and my phone rings. I see it's the manager I interviewed with a few weeks earlier. He tells me, "It's a really tough decision, but they decided to go with another candidate." My heart cracks open all over again. This was my ticket to have it all—a full-time job and being closer to the grandkids . . . now what?

In my heart, I know this wasn't the right decision for me at this time. Not getting this transfer wakes me up and lets me know that I must get things in order with my life before moving forward. So that is exactly what I do, I get things in order.

A year later, I am looking at the company's newsletter. There is a short story about the person who got the job instead of me. It says she got a promotion. *Oh my gosh, is that job I applied to before posted again?*

Sure enough, I look at their job postings and it is. I speak to the manager and ask, "Can I apply for the job again?" He gives me his blessing. So, I do.

Within a month, I interview for the job, I'm given an offer that I accept, and am planning the move. I move to a home a few hours from my son and my daughter. Visits are much more frequent, and I am not using as much vacation time with each visit. I attend ball games, dance recitals, and educational functions, and most importantly, my grandkids know who Grandma Nae is and that she knows them.

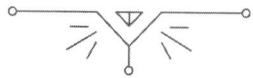

My Dream to Wear Pumps

Cynthia D. Lamberth
FLORIDA, USA

Today, I am on the city bus headed downtown for a fun day of window shopping with my friends. I notice most people on the bus wear shoes like my parents—the steel-toed boots of a factory or construction worker, or the white shoes of a healthcare worker.

However, people's shoes are different in the heart of downtown where there are office buildings, department stores, and restaurants. I see many young women in suits and dresses with matching pumps. I want this well-dressed, pump-wearing dream. I am trying to figure out what these sharply-dressed women do, and I know I want to look like that; happy, out having lunch with girlfriends, and wearing a pretty suit with matching pumps!

Many days, I slide my feet into pumps from my mom's closet, creating noise-clacking strides on the hardwood floors, pretending to head out to my job in a downtown office building. This is my dream.

Fast forward, and it's the summer before my senior year in high school. I am sitting on the floor of our kitchen crying, as I have just hung up the phone after speaking with a boyfriend who told me that, as a college man, he had moved on. I feel rejected, unworthy, alone, and sad that our relationship is over.

Back on my kitchen floor, I look up and realize someone is watching. My great aunt is arranging her favorite white roses in a vase. She motions for me to come and sit with her. I expect the comforting hug; however, this feisty, self-made great aunt, visiting from afar, tells me I have a decision to make. I can decide how I am thinking and feeling about that call. She also encourages me to think of a future that is not dependent on the acceptance of a boy or my friends.

She asks, "What would you love?" I thought about the pumps, but I knew she was asking, "What do you want to be when you grow up?" As the editor of the high school yearbook, the profession of journalist seems valid, even though I have no idea how I will do it.

My dear Great Aunt Odie asks, "Do you believe you can be a star journalist?" I'm not sure. I know I want to wear pumps and have lunch with girlfriends . . . and she says, "I am sure you can." She can see me flying to a city where I am covering a big convention or meeting, so that the world will know about the information covered and the decisions made.

I ask her many questions about flying and writing. She fills in many details from her experiences. I love the details about writing stories, telling people about things that are important to them, and writing stories in ways that touch people's hearts, or stir their curiosity.

So I, this girl with four homemade outfits for the five-day school week, who doesn't have a suit or pumps, now have a vision and can see how that might be my future.

Great Aunt Odie makes me a generous offer. If I keep my

grades up and apply to college, she will send me the tuition money at the end of each college quarter. In addition, she asks that I send her my grades, write her letters, send her writing samples, and work to pay for books and food to hold up my end of the agreement. And I agree.

What a gift! But more than the gift of the tuition is the gift of her believing in me. She speaks possibility into me. I decide to change my life; I have a dream and a vision of my future.

When it's time, I head to college. I write stories for my aunt, send her my Dean's List grades, and hone my writing and leadership skills serving in the student government association as the Pan Hellenic president, special needs orientation leader, and academic council. The vision of my career evolves from journalist to writer, speaker, and facilitator.

My Great Aunt Odie left this earthly existence during my second year of college, and I miss sending her my writing and talking to her about my plans. I also miss the checks to help me with school; however, based on her belief that has now become my belief and vision, I work several jobs at a time to earn my first degree.

My first professional job after my undergraduate degree is a writing position downtown in a large office building. I wear suits and pumps to work! A painting of white roses my Great Aunt Odie created hangs in my office. It's as if she is always looking over my shoulder—shining her good counsel down on me.

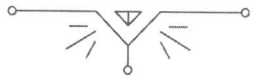

Ask a Different Question

Gael Hogan
CANADA

Grasping Mike's hand, dread constricting my body, I force myself to look at my doctor. She focuses her full attention on us. Her eyes tear up.

"The biopsy shows that you have (words I can't understand) carcinoma."

Breast cancer.

Mike and I clutch each other's hands more tightly, seeking comfort.

We are terrified.

In the days after my diagnosis, my mind spins in disbelief and confusion. I find myself wondering, "What am I doing wrong?"

This past year and a half, my art has been featured in five art shows and two craft fairs. I'm finally living my dream of being an artist after a lifetime of hesitating and feeling "not quite ready." This amazing progress has inspired me. I feel so alive, so fulfilled. And my progress has ignited the fire of a new passion—to empower others to live their dreams. I have become a Life Coach and even enrolled my first client. Now, I wonder how I will fulfill my commitment to him while going through cancer treatment.

"How can this be happening to me?"

I have eaten blueberries every day for years. I take Vitamin D. I exercise religiously.

"Am I going to die?"

Spinning with fear and confusion, I bring these questions to my own coach.

"What am I doing wrong?" I ask her. I am frantic, trying to understand. She listens, and then she gives me some of the best advice I've ever received.

"First of all," she suggests, "ask a different question."

"Like what?" I wonder, confused.

"Start asking, what would you love?" she advises.

Desperate to make sense of this nightmare, I ask myself, "What would I love?"

The answers float into my mind. I would love to be in vibrant health. I would love to live through this experience. I'd love to live near both my beautiful daughters and be involved and important in the lives of my grandchildren. I would love for Mike and me to own a cottage on a lake. It would be amazing to take my grandchildren paddling in my kayak. I'd love to have art shows in galleries and sell my paintings to art lovers and tourists. I'd love to coach people and help empower them to live their dreams.

I would love to live.

My coach offers me more advice. "Lean into gratitude," she suggests.

This seems very challenging right now. "Really?"

"I know you're not grateful that you have cancer, but look

around your life and find things you are grateful for. Write them down every day."

I do.

Before long, I have filled a whole notebook. I begin to realize there really is an abundance of good in my life. So many things bring me joy and comfort. I am grateful.

Her last words of advice are, "Look for the gifts and the learning."

This idea seems impossible, but I keep asking for the gift to show itself.

Exactly one month after receiving the news that I have cancer, I find myself hugging Mike and turning to walk alone into a sterile, bright, operating room. I shiver in the coldness of the room. But the coldness melts into kindness as my surgeon, a wonderful, gentle man, introduces me to his team, as if we are all at a dinner party. He will do his best to save my life.

Showering after the mastectomy is challenging. I must avoid getting the dressing wet. Towelling off after my shower, I catch my reflection in the mirror. Tears slide down my cheeks.

"How could I allow them to do this to me?"

I hear a knock on the bathroom door. The next thing I know, Mike is wrapping me in his arms. He soothes away the tears and grief.

When I meet with my surgeon three weeks later, he is delighted. The mastectomy was a complete success! He tells me he "got it all" and pronounces me "cancer free."

Unsure, dazed, I walk into the nearby washroom and look into the eyes of my reflection in the mirror.

"I get to live?" I ask my reflection.

"You get to live."

But I have many months of treatment ahead of me to ensure this prognosis comes true.

My oncologist prescribes three chemo drugs, plus a bag full of other drugs to deal with all the side effects. I create a schedule to keep track of it all. I am now a walking pharmacy.

I get weaker with each chemo treatment. My hair falls out in handfuls. Mike comes with me for walks, to keep me on my feet. My anxiety and reluctance intensify with each chemo treatment, tightening my gut and chest like a vice-grip. Sometimes all I can do is breathe, as the poisonous medicine floods my body.

Yet, I continue to use the precious tools from my coach. They become my lifeline. Resting on my bed, gazing out the window, I ask myself, "What would I love? What am I grateful for?" The answers calm my anxiety and ease my fear; they bring me peace and hope.

I imagine myself at the cottage we would love to own. On the beach in the early morning, the water is like glass. My little grandson, in his tiny lifejacket, "helps" me drag my kayak down to the lake. We climb in; he sits in front of me as I paddle through the still clear water. Fish jump to catch bugs on the surface of the lake. An eagle dives, right in front of us. It splashes into the water and rises up again with a fish in its talons. My grandson is mesmerized. He can't stop talking about it as we glide along. In the reeds nearby we hear the soulful call of the loons. I feel happy and vibrantly healthy, filled with gratitude to be alive.

It is two and a half years since my mastectomy. We decide to brave the summer heat and hike with good friends through a beautiful old-growth forest. The goal, a cool and refreshing waterfall. The rosemary scent of the trees fills my nostrils. I feel so alive!

It's November. My car has disappeared under the snow. We have sold our house. This place is now littered with piles of things to be packed or donated, as we prepare for "the long drive" to the east coast. Soon, I'll be kissing my grandson's chubby cheeks.

No time now to finish the new painting I started. That will happen in my new studio.

We will start cottage-hunting in the spring.

This is truly living. I love my life.

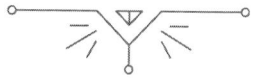

From Fear to Thriving

Donald E. Brunnert

TEXAS, USA

Since moving to Dallas, Texas, in 1997 from a small rural area outside of St. Louis, Missouri, I have lived a childhood dream of being in a city with unlimited freedoms and opportunities. Since moving to Dallas, I have spent over nineteen years building a successful career in our software development division.

Fast forward to October 2015—I woke up that morning with the same routine, headed to Starbuck's for a latté and breakfast, and went to work. The discussions leading up to this week had focused on the next round of layoffs. Since tens of thousands of employees had been impacted over the past decade, it was no surprise that we all were chatting about which organization, departments, and teams would be affected next.

What I didn't expect on this very typical day was to realize that one other teammate and I were notified to be at the office the following day at 8:00 AM and 8:30 AM, respectively. I was worried and concerned as the day slowly dragged along, and that worry only intensified throughout the evening.

I began to reflect on my life and what I and Jason, my partner of four years, had created since merging our lives. We had recently sold my condo and moved into our spacious two-bedroom, two-bath apartment while searching for a home to buy. It would be our first home purchase together. We had nice cars, nice clothes, and two spoiled dogs. We lived a block from stores, restaurants, and bars, where we walked almost every evening to enjoy the nightlife. By all accounts, we were living privileged lives and were so grateful. I didn't want any of that to change.

I woke up that morning preparing myself for the in-person 8:00 AM meeting. Walking into the dimly lit conference room, I felt a shortness of breath and I was starting to sweat. Once my boss quickly introduced herself and our HR partner, I could barely understand the rest of the conversation.

My mind was racing while she explained I was being let go, "How, after twenty years, are you doing this to me?" I thought. My boss was someone with whom I had a close relationship personally and professionally, having worked together for years. I felt betrayed and hurt and couldn't understand how this was happening. As the meeting continued, my boss explained my severance package. I had some questions: "Why were they not taking care of me as they had during so many other layoffs? What was the reason no one had even given me a heads-up?"

As she ended the meeting, I made my way down to my office and saw the blurred faces of everyone around me in my dazed confusion. I gathered a few of the items I had brought that morning and left without any of us speaking to one another.

Over the next several months, my now husband and I moved down the hall to the smallest one-bedroom, one-bath apartment to finish our lease agreement. I started thinking of every bill and where every dollar was going, as we had to downsize our lives. The small space added to my growing despair. I thought I would like to know if I could do something to start my own business. Where should I look for work? Did I even want to look for work?

Still, our strained situation only added to the devastation of our sudden losses; my mother-in-law had passed from ovarian cancer, and our sweet dogs, Amelia, at the age of sixteen, and Nevin, at the age of nine, had died. Now my career seemed to be dead as well.

January 1st, 2016, my ninety days to find a job within the company are over without an offer, and this is my last day. I'm turning in my badge. It is a dark day, and I feel empty; my feelings only worsen when I realize no one said farewell. No one offered any words of encouragement. As I am driving out of the darkness from the dingy underground parking garage and watching the steel gate close behind me in the rear-view mirror, I feel a sense of relief, which is entirely unexpected.

Six months later, our family was in a downsized condo with two downsized practical cars and a growing fear of what would be next. Having lost a twenty-year career left me wondering about my future. I wanted to return to a sociable work environment and earn an income. However, shortly after that, a friend recommended me for a job. I interviewed and got the job. I was still longing for something more challenging and was discontented not to be earning the kind of money I had made in my previous career.

This disappointment began to affect my home life. My despair seemed overwhelming, even to the point of affecting my relationship with my husband. Fortunately, to my amazement, a close friend recommended a Chakra Cleanse, as it had helped correct her feelings of imbalance. A series of events began that I had never believed possible. I was meditating and having weekly sessions and noticed some minor changes.

As the summer of 2017 approached, I exchanged an email with a recruiter looking for contractors for a technology company—work like my prior experience. The recruiter and I fostered a four-year relationship. I began working contracts in new industries that I never knew were possible.

These serendipitous moments opened new areas of my life, but as time passed, I felt myself slipping back into despair. I was having trouble in my relationship with my husband and noticed similar problems in relationships around me. Fortunately, to my surprise, a close friend reached out to let us know she had launched a new life coaching business and believed we would benefit. My husband and I reluctantly started with her. The program included a deep study and immersion into our love, relationships, and time and money issues. Unexpectedly, we saw the Universe conspiring to move us toward our dreams.

Our lives continued to morph in the direction of our dreams as we studied. I could not imagine our tiny one-bedroom condo would upgrade to a three-story home. Nor could I suspect that our practical cars would upgrade to luxury cars. I went from having no job to working full-time in an amazing organization.

The exciting part is that changing taught me that stepping into the fear of a career in a new industry was freeing. I now understand that I need to grow, learn, and transform daily to live by design. I am grateful for every day I take a breath.

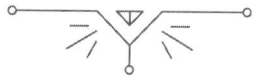

Light After the Storm

Jason Brumfield

TEXAS, USA

"If you plan to stay, you better put an ax in the attic so you can break through the roof when the water rises." The meteorologist's warning is quite clear—*when*, not *if.*

I have always been a creature of habit who finds solace in familiarity and routines; change and I do not make the best companions. My comfort zone is my world, so imagine what happens when my comfort zone comes face-to-face with one of the largest natural disasters this country has ever seen.

The minimal hurricane that had cut across the southern part of Florida Friday morning is now heading our way. New Orleans is in the center of Hurricane Katrina's bullseye. We have less than 48 hours to decide whether we should ride it out or seek shelter out of the storm's reach.

At first, I'm not worried. The forecast is always gloom and doom when storms enter the Gulf, but they always turn, and we only get a little rain. But as Katrina maintains a steady course and begins picking up speed, I begin to panic. There is a 20-foot wall of water heading toward a city that sits below sea level. Math is not my strong point, but I understand that the waterline would be well above my head. Decision made—it's time to leave. The plan is to meet at my parents' house Sunday morning, and I will follow them to Dallas.

This isn't my first evacuation. For Gulf Coast residents, evacuations are unexpected "vacations." After a couple of days, we return home, clean up a few fallen branches, then comfortably slip back into our daily routines. But something feels dreadfully different this time. My gut tells me that this will be no vacation. How long will we be gone? How much damage will the storm do? Twenty feet is *a lot* of water! What about my career? I've just had the best first week of school in my six-year teaching career. Will I have to start over? Many questions, no answers. I have never experienced uncertainty like this before.

Before joining my parents, I take one last drive around the city. There is an eerie stillness over the French Quarter this morning. Anyone familiar with the Quarter knows there is a constant throng of tourists and revelers in its jazz-soaked streets. Today, the streets are empty, and the only sound heard is the distant whirring of power tools as residents make last-minute preparations to secure their property from the monster storm, the first rainbands of which are now passing overhead.

We finally make it to Dallas around sunrise the next day. After checking into our two-bedroom hotel suite, we turn on the television to see how our city fared. We see people walking down familiar streets through ankle-deep water. Ankle deep is nowhere near the predicted 20 feet. The news is promising. The storm turned slightly east, sparing New Orleans a direct hit. Maybe we can head home in a couple of days and get back to our lives. With a sense of relief, I allow myself to drift to sleep.

When I awaken, I rub my eyes to make sure I'm not still dreaming because what I am now seeing on the television is a nightmare. The levees broke. About 80% of the city is filled with water. People are on rooftops, desperate for help. Hope for a quick return home fades. This is disastrous. Now I must figure out how to navigate the uncertainty that Katrina has left behind.

Days turn into weeks. My emotions linger on the heavier side of hopelessness and grief. I crave normalcy. Living out of a suitcase in a hotel room stresses me, so I sign a month-to-month lease for an apartment (my parents do the same, a couple of doors down from me). No matter how many fleur-de-lis pictures I hang on the wall, it's just not home. I feel lost, like I'm merely going through the motions. And I am jealous of all of the people around me who are going about their everyday lives. To them it's an ordinary Thursday; to me it's another day added onto a never-ending sentence for a crime I didn't commit.

One mid-September morning, I am watching a news story where storm survivors discuss what life in New Orleans was like in the days after the storm. That's when it hits me: I am fortunate. Over 1000 people lost their lives to Katrina. Thousands more lost everything they owned. Many people were stranded for days with no food or drinkable water. Yes, I'm experiencing a major disruption in my life, but I'm alive. My family and I are safe. My friends, though scattered across the country, are safe. I decide to let go of the hopelessness that has weighed me down. I decide to find the rainbow at the end of the storm.

Never had I imagined living anywhere besides NOLA, but as I start looking beyond my circumstances, I see the opportunity for a new life in Dallas. I have an apartment; that's a start. I just need a job. I apply for teaching positions across the Metroplex. It's not long before I get a call from the associate principal at the high school near my apartment. Student enrollment is up after the hurricane, and the school wants to schedule an interview with me. I am elated as I hang up the phone.

My comfort zone decides to protest my decision to remain in Dallas. This interview makes things real; a job is a long-term commitment. "Things might get better back home and you can return to your old life," my comfort zone says. I ask the Universe for a sign. When I go out onto the patio to get some air, I hear the flutter of wings above my head. A cardinal perches on the fence. This isn't just a sign, it's a flashing billboard. The school where I am interviewing—their mascot is the Cardinal!

A week later, my interview ends with a job offer and a handshake. This moment would forever change the trajectory of my career in education, giving me opportunities that eventually led me from the classroom to leadership roles at Central Office. Although I still appreciate familiarity and routines in my daily life, when it comes to opportunities, I've grown quite comfortable stepping out of my comfort zone. If I learned anything from my experience with Hurricane Katrina, it's that life puts you exactly where you need to be, exactly when you need to be there. You just have to be willing to step into it.

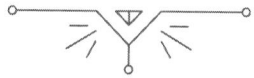

Lessons on Healing
from Life's Challenges

Aurelie Catherine Cormier
MASSACHUSETTS, USA

A message flashed across my work phone. "Your new admission is here." She is a young woman newly diagnosed with lymphoma. We are preparing for her first cycle of chemotherapy. So many ideas go through my mind. I know that this is often a difficult road. Through it all, I am always trying to figure out what makes the difference, how I can empower my patients to reach toward their dreams. My patients have taught me as much as I hope I have taught them about survivorship. I wondered what this young woman's journey would be. As a young nurse, I felt the medications and treatments made the difference. As an experienced nurse, with my own health challenges of hypertension, glaucoma and exposure to DDT in my youth, what I know for sure is that, in many situations, when patients take control and decide to make major changes in their lifestyle earlier in the course of their illness, this can create the best outcomes. I remind myself I can only empower what patients desire through their own dreams. I reviewed my list of what I needed to complete for her admission and how I may empower her for the treatment ahead as I worked my way towards her room. As I walked in, I took a deep breath and thought, "focus on healing." She was setting up the few belongings she had brought with her. I introduced myself and briefly explained the process.

I asked the routine admission questions. She was bright and seemed to have a moderately healthy lifestyle. We went through her current symptoms leading up to her diagnosis as well as her general habits. I asked her to think about any toxic environmental exposures in her home, work or play. I started with her home, "Anything you can think of?"

"No," she responded. I asked about her yard.

"No."

"Any chemicals on the lawn?" I asked. She said they had a landscaping company that took care of the lawn, so, no. Then she hesitated with what seemed like a long pause.

"Well, now that you mention it, I am the one that takes care of the weeds in the yard," she said. She went on to explain that she would put a chemical on the weeds to kill them twice a year. I explained to her that it would be important for her to not only stop using the chemical but avoid spraying any chemicals on her lawn and being aware of her environment in general. I explained that we could give her the six chemotherapy treatments which are the gold standard regimen for her type of lymphoma, but that continued exposure to these chemicals could undo the benefit she would be getting from the treatment. I encouraged her to take an inventory of her environment and try to minimize any toxic exposure, especially within her home. She listened.

Three weeks later, as I was in the middle of my shift, she ran up to me with excitement and exclaimed, "Guess what I did? I gave away that bag you suggested." We both smiled.

"That is wonderful news," I said. I was so happy for her and felt that she was motivated to make changes in her life to give herself the best chance of responding to the chemotherapy treatment. I knew that this was not easy, but I sensed that she was motivated to do whatever she could to get better, step by step.

The next cycle, one of my colleagues tells me my patient is experiencing a complication of her treatment. I check in with her and she explains what is happening. I can hear that she is distressed and scared about the long-term implications of these complications. Fortunately, I know that she is surrounded by an expert team working hard to get her through this very intense regimen. I visit her as much as I can to offer support.

Several months later, she completes her chemotherapy and I am comforted to know that despite feeling tired and worn down, she looks well overall. Her follow-up testing shows that she responded to her treatment. She asks questions and enjoys hearing whatever she can do to help. I share with her what I have learned that can make a difference for many chronic illnesses, as I have slowly transformed my own health using many of these strategies. It is a process, and I have found that every improvement helps me feel better. I relay to this woman that receiving the best-evidence treatment for her particular lymphoma is highly important, but I assure her that equally important is eating a wholesome, nutrient-dense diet, going organic as much as possible, getting 20–30 minutes of aerobic exercise a day, getting adequate sleep, being surrounded with positive relationships, managing stress and switching from potentially harmful products to non-toxic ones like vinegar and baking soda, glass over plastic, filtered water and minimizing chemicals in the home. She tells me that despite the fact that her husband travels a lot for his work, they have started going out for walks together as much as possible and, when he is not there, she walks at least two miles a day. I have a good feeling about her over-all outcome. She is working toward each of these survival strategies by focusing on one at a time.

She also shares with me that this experience has helped her reassess her priorities. She found a job that she would love, but is unsure if she will get it. She wants to do something different, and I have seen how well she has navigated her diagnosis, undergoing the chemotherapy, dealing with the complications and being very motivated to do whatever she can to give her body the best chance of healing. I tell her that she needs to focus on her own healing first, but I absolutely sense that when the time is right, she has so much insight, compassion and wisdom to share with people that I think she would be the perfect person for this position.

Five years later, after her appointment with her Primary Oncologist, we get together and she shares the good news with me. She tells me that her doctor told her all her scans show that there is no evidence of lymphoma. She can consider herself cured now. I feel a deep sense of joy for her. Healing from health challenges is possible, and she is the one who is making the difference one step at a time!

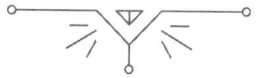

What If I Can?

Lin Yuan-Su
CANADA

It's February, and I live in Canada. That's why I'm wearing my winter jacket as I sit inside Sister Margaret's office, bawling my eyes out.

I'm crying so hard that I'm hunched over. My face is buried in the folds of my jacket.

Sister Margaret is a petite lady. She wears short, curly hair and glasses that seem too big for her face. As I sob, she allows me to have this moment. All she does is reach over and pat my back.

I'm not sure why I've chosen to cry in her office. To be honest, I don't even know what she teaches at the university. All I know is that her office is always open to students, whether they need someone to confide in or just want to have a conversation with an adult.

And so, here I am. Sitting and sobbing. In despair. Feeling like my world has ended.

Last week, I was on cloud nine, thanks to an email I received on Friday. It told me that my academic dreams were coming true. I had been accepted into the Master of Science in Food and Nutrition program!

For over a year, I had busted my butt for this. I chased and mastered every qualification I would need. Good grades. A high GPA. Volunteer experience. Leadership experience. Work experience.

Throughout this journey, I kept bumping into one phrase: You can't.

You can't do this because you're an international student.

You can't do this because your English is just not good enough.

You can't do this because you don't have any nutrition-related experience.

Nobody said these things to my face, but I could tell that this was what they were thinking. They weren't being mean. And, in their own way, they wanted the best for me. It's just that they simply didn't believe that I could do this.

Yet, every time I encountered, "You can't," I asked myself a question: What if I can?

If I don't try, I thought, then they're right. I can't. So: what if I can?

Am I going to hurt anyone if I do try? I pondered. So: what if I can?

I just kept wondering, What if I can? And that question kept me going.

It had kept me going through every step of this highly competitive process: the application, the study, the volunteering, the interviews. All the way until last Friday, when the official email finally delivered my answer: Yes, you can!

However, I have just discovered there's a big BUT in my way. This particular program doesn't offer any academic funding or financial support to students. I am responsible for all my tuition and personal living expenses.

Now, my mind is stuck. No, you can't, it says. You can't afford this. In fact, the phrase "I can't" hangs like a neon sign above my head. It's an ugly, dingy, glaring sign, and it fills me with pain. I feel like I'm falling all the way to the bottom of a deep, dark hole.

This falling sensation has led me here, to Sister Margaret's office. I didn't plan to break down, but I just can't help it. So I sob, and sob, and sob.

Because I'm hunched over, I don't see Sister Margaret reach for me. Her touch is unexpected, and immediately, I feel something different. I feel a sensation of calmness. A sensation of love. And I'm confused. I hardly know Sister Margaret. She doesn't know me that well, either. How can her soft touch inspire these sensations?

With Sister Margaret's help, it takes me about ten minutes to calm down. She doesn't give me any life-changing advice or magical solutions. She simply says, "It will all work out." And then she says it again, her hand still on my shoulder.

I don't believe her. I still believe in the flashing neon sign that screams above my head. I can't have my dream, because I don't have the money. Because my parents can't scrape up the money. Because the university won't give me the money. These are the reasons that I can't.

Still, with Sister Margaret's presence, I feel strong enough to stand up, thank her for her love, and carry on with my day.

Out in the hallway, I stop and lean against the corner. It's about time for the next round of classes to start. Crowds of students bustle past me. I know that my face is red and puffy from crying. It must be frightful. The others are probably wondering what's wrong with me.

But at this moment, as I watch the students walking past, I'm suddenly struck with calmness and pride. Wow, I think to myself. I did it. I actually did it. Through my entire journey, so many people told me that I can't. But I didn't give up. Instead, I questioned their beliefs. I kept wondering about what I *can* do.

My thought train continues, picking up steam. Am I going to let the money stuff stop me? Really? Seriously? And I begin talking at myself. Are you going to allow this money thing to prove that everyone else was right? That you can't? Well, what if you can?

As if struck by lightning, my whole demeanor changes. A boost of confidence shoots through me. Sister Margaret is right. Everything is going to work out.

Do I know how? Heck no! Yet, when I once again ask myself the question—What if I can?—I get a clear answer. A calm answer. A tried-and-true answer. Yes, I can. So I walk down the hall and leave the building. There's more of this day left to live.

A week later, my phone rings. When I answer, I'm surprised to hear the voice of a hospital HR officer. We'd met a few months back, when I was applying for a job that I knew they wouldn't offer to me.

Now, he tells me that they want to hire me to be, of all things, a supervisor. I'm stunned, almost speechless at this incredible offer. It's a real job that pays a generous wage.

When I end the call, I can't stop smiling. This one job won't cover all of my Master's education expenses. But that doesn't matter. I know the Universe is not done yet.

I wonder what can I do next?

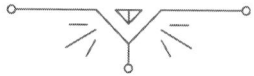

You're Too Old

Pat Acklie-Roth

TEXAS, USA

December, 2016 and my husband John and I are in the ER, he with high blood pressure. It hasn't come down after three nitro pills. X-rays are taken. We're told his lungs look terrible. Three days later, the specialist says John has Interstitial Fibrosis Lung Disease. It's incurable, and the doctor prescribes medicine to stop the progression. They give him three years to live. Other medicines are added, but he gets worse.

By 2017, he's on oxygen most of the time, getting weaker, and we decide to ask the doctor about a lung transplant. He goes to the appointment and I go to work. I come home and he's sitting in the living room with a strange look on his face. At today's appointment he was told that at 70 he's "too old" for a lung transplant. The pulmonologist said, "When you get tired, let me know, we will take you off of your meds and call in Hospice." He says he is forty shades of depressed hearing this and is not ready to accept it. John is always an upbeat and happy soul. I have never heard him say he was depressed. This is a death sentence to him. He was put on medicine from Germany costing $1,800 a month to slow the progression down, but he is deteriorating.

It's September 2019, and we seek a second opinion at UT Southwestern in Dallas, Texas, one of the top transplant hospitals in the United States. They have to know he is a good candidate for the transplant, that his age will not stop it. He is tested thoroughly for everything imaginable, even his eyes and teeth, and he passes with flying colors. He's told to lose 30 pounds and loses 40. Our spirits are lifted and we have renewed hope.

We left my 97-year-old mom in Nebraska because she insisted I had to be with John. She loves him and understands the seriousness of his disease. We head back to Nebraska to close my sewing business, but we're told to get back to Texas ASAP. I rush to finish orders and pack, and we're back in Texas in a week. We have no idea how long we will have to wait for a matching donor, possibly months, or even years. We spend one week at a hotel, but then are given a small apartment, and we only have to pay the electricity and cable. A gentleman who received a heart transplant built the apartments and set eight units aside to be rent free for transplant patients to wait and to recover, and we can stay as long as we need to.

Monday, we're in the apartment. Tired, I make the bed and say I will put things away tomorrow. Tuesday, at 4:50 AM, John's phone rings. He's not wearing his hearing aids, so I shake him awake, saying, "Your phone, your phone!" It's the hospital. We're told, "Get here ASAP." We arrive, and are told there is a donor, but that everything must match, tissue, blood, everything! If they get into the surgery and even one thing doesn't match, everything stops and we wait for another call. He is prepped and Wednesday morning he's in surgery. I wait for the nurse to call with updates. She calls and says, "It's a go!" Oh my God! Tears come to my eyes. I wait. He is in God's hands now!

I pray for John, the doctors, and the nurses. His doctor is new to Dallas. It's her first surgery here, although she was head of transplants in California and has a new procedure. In the waiting room, I meet the wife of the man receiving John's donor's heart. John is receiving the right lung and another person the left lung. Many lives are saved today because of the donor family. Watching the news, we learn a young construction worker was hit and killed by a drunk driver. God works in mysterious ways and I can't help but wonder.

Six hours later, John is back in his room hooked up to lots of machines and tubes. I can't go into his room for three days, but look through the glass. The doctor said he may not recognize me for a couple of days. He sees me on the other side of the glass, gives me his sweet smile, and waves. He remembered me! They watch him closely, and eight days after surgery, he is released with no oxygen, but has a feeding tube in his nose because he has a hiatal hernia. We were initially told he would be in the hospital for four weeks.

There are many trips to the doctor's office, as she monitors him closely. He's on lots of anti-rejection medications through the feeding tube, along with his liquid food. On one of our trips, we get to meet the wonderful gentleman who received the left lung, Tommy, and his sweet wife, Diane. There is an instant bond with them that we treasure.

I learn to give shots, crush meds and give liquid food in the feeding tube. Several times, the tube plugs. Sometimes I am able to clear it, but twice we have to go to the ER to have them do it. We are grateful for the doctors, to God and to the unselfish donor family for giving my sweet John new life.

February, and a call comes that my mom has cancer. John's sisters stay with him. He can't stay by himself or drive to doctors' appointments. I drive to Nebraska, where I spend Mom's last two weeks with her and take care of the funeral. I am so grateful to have that precious time with her to her end. Then, I drive back to my sweet John in Texas.

March 2020, and the hernia surgery is done. John can eat soft foods and starts walking outside. He develops pneumonia and is back in the hospital for a few days.

In April, he's cleared to travel back to Nebraska. In October, we travel to our home in Pharr, Texas. November brings COVID to John and me. He is life-flighted to Dallas for 10 days; then it's back to Pharr and to Nebraska in April.

We make many follow-up visits to Dallas, but also travel 50,000 miles in our motorhome, going whenever we can during this precious time. I'm doing my life coaching on the road; we stay at truck stops and see family and our friends, Alice and Ben. In July 2022, we attend our grandson Logan and his bride Kaitlyn's wedding in St. Augustine, Florida. John is feeling so good, dancing with me to "Shout," "YMCA," and the Congo Line. It's great and such a blessing to be able to have this time with him, the love of my life, my sweet John, who it turned out was "not too old!"

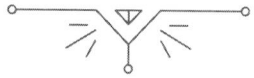

Stardust Synchronicities and One . . . Singular Sensation

Ryan Christopher Harris Olssen

NEVADA, USA

Is 11 stories high enough? Better make it 20 stories just in case. I cannot help thinking dark thoughts even while overlooking the crystal blue Caribbean Sea in an awesome ocean-front Santa Marta, Colombia, Airbnb. Why am I still unable to get my own mind right after dedicating over a year of my life to being a mindset coach? Haven't I faced enough storms to deserve things finally being easier?

Am I a fraud . . . selling inspiring results to others when I have not fully experienced them for myself first? I am consumed by questions that overload my mind, including the biggest one of all . . . will I decide on suicide, or keep trying to overcome my failures to succeed?

I feel the most alone I have ever felt in my entire life, having nobody I can turn to in this moment. After all, I am supposed to be the one leading people to create and live a life they love. What will people think or say when my most private thoughts get out? How would my existing clients react if they found out I was so close to committing suicide?

From the outside, people see me as the walking definition of positivity, many close to me even calling me painfully positive, but now I only feel discouragement, guilt and shame inside my very heavy heart. Have I learned nothing these past 20 years from when I was successful in life? What am I missing? I have tried everything my first mentor (a master sports psychologist) taught me to succeed, and I have since improved my abilities by applying what my current mentors have taught me.

My time in the Sports Betting and Casino Industry inspired my willingness to go after my latest dreams in a big way. My gambler's mindset is all I have in this moment, because going to church growing up taught me a lot about religion, but very little about Faith. I search deep inside for at least one way I won't run out of money, but my worst doubts keep me believing that killing myself is my best option when the money runs out.

Suddenly my mind turns to my favorite movie of all time, "It's A Wonderful Life." I have always tried to be like Jimmy Stewart's character George Bailey, and now I find myself following the same thoughts he had when facing a big money problem. In the movie, George Bailey's life or death money problem led him to plan to jump off Bedford Falls Bridge. He was choosing suicide too, for what he believed to be the best solution for everyone involved . . . even his wife and four young children.

Just before he jumped, his guardian angel saved him, but that was a movie! There are no guardian angels in real life. Are there? I am now questioning and challenging every belief I have ever had. I feel I owe it to myself to double check every possibility one last time before I go. My thoughts lead me to remember how suicide has already featured in my family's history.

This curiosity distracts me enough from using a permanent

choice to solve a temporary problem; I might be solving one problem but creating more problems for many others. Finally, my own guardian angel shows up for me . . . mine in the form of an inner voice I hear from the deepest part of my heart. It whispers a suggestion to me. "Before you give up for good, Ryan, you should probably talk to at least one other person about this."

I decide to call upon a most near and dear mentor before my suicidal thoughts take hold once again. I don't know how to deal with them . . . keep suppressing them and ignoring them or confront them head-on. With her help, I regain my courage to face these feelings and fears, only to find my greatest freedom and joy is just on the other side of my biggest fear.

I begin seeing signs and miracles all around me. I reconnect with the parts of my life that have brought me the most joy up until now. I embrace the part of me that has put so much effort into pursuing what I would love, and my eyes are now open to what has prevented me from being successful this time. I have been thinking I must do everything alone and without help from anyone or anything. I also realize I never truly believed my current efforts would ever pay off.

My "make it happen" mantra has held me back this entire time, and in this moment of clarity my mantra shifts to "make it welcome," practicing the art of "doing, by not doing." I remember rest is as important as work. Growing my believing power and faith in what's possible is the other part of the secret.

On reflection I see how my faith constantly spoke to me through Stardust Synchronicities (meaningful coincidences), saying life has always had *much* bigger plans for me. Plans I could not see until I healed several parts of my past and began living my truth.

Through Stardust signs from New York to California and of

course the iconic Stardust on the Las Vegas Strip, I am directed to what thrills and fulfills me in this life. Just like the implosion of Vegas's Stardust, my life has similarly transformed into a better reality. My faith inspires me to forever release suicide as an option in my life and instead discover new truths with a ten-year experiment to unlock more of my hidden potential. I now make my choices through what consciously feels expansive to me, no longer basing my decisions on what other people might think or say.

Thanks to five cherished romantic relationships with two significant girlfriends, two fiancées and one amazing marriage blessing me with two bonus kids and much more, I am intentionally choosing to be One Singular Sensation, showing my love in the ways I *love*, which means releasing romantic relationships.

In their place, I am leaning more into my deep love of my family, friends, professional contacts, and my love that desires the very best for their entire families. I now feel most divinely aligned as I live equally for mind, body, soul and loved ones. Life keeps providing me even greater abundance, all while I am living how I desire.

In this experimental decade, I also release alcohol, caffeinated drinks, chocolate, controlled substances, gambling, and pork products. What experiments will you do to unlock your hidden potential?

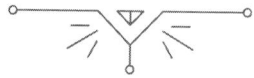

When Pain Pushed Me to Make a Change

Fadia Soueidan
MICHIGAN, USA

I worked as a Respiratory Therapist for over 13 years. Being a Respiratory Therapist is one of the most rewarding careers, in my mind. Health care in general is a rewarding field for those who are in it for the right reasons.

As Respiratory Therapists, we are often pulled in many different directions. We are spread very thin, and we do a lot of running around. It was worth every step for me because I felt like I was actually making a difference, until I wasn't. My health was deteriorating, my relationships were suffering, and I began to feel depleted on all levels. But was I depleted enough to walk away from a career that I absolutely loved in the midst of a pandemic?

It was a Friday evening; I was driving into work, and as soon as I approached the parking structure I began to feel sick. My stomach was bubbling, and my heart started racing. I put down the window, thinking maybe I just needed fresh air. As soon as I went up the ramp I threw up all over my car and all over my scrubs. I panicked and struggled to get into a parking spot safely. My first thought was shoot, now I'm going to be late. I called shift lead and explained my situation. She reassured me that everything would be okay, and that if I didn't feel sick and wanted to stay I could because we had two call-offs and were short-staffed again that night. That night I ended up working in the medical unit. I had 16 vented patients, all very critical. That night I took two of my most critical patients who were connected to ventilators on travels, one to get a CT scan and the other one to MRI. As soon as I got back I got to terminally wean a patient that I had taken care of for quite some time. I didn't have enough time to begin to process that loss before I found myself coding three patients back to back to back. At the end of the third code, I stood there motionless, feeling numb. I had done everything I could and it was not enough. I was not saving anyone, and I was losing my health in the process.

That morning I cried. I cried all the way home, feeling lost and hopeless. The images of all the events within the last 12 hours had me shaking and feeling so cold. I had dealt with patients passing away before, and I had had my fair share of similarly bad nights. But this time I knew something had to change. I was working harder than anyone I knew and getting none of the results I wanted in any area of my life. That's when I decided to put together my resignation letter and shortly after submitted my two-week notice. And as soon as I submitted it, fear rose up and took over my whole being. There was a huge part of me arguing for why I couldn't quit, for why this was not the right time. For why this was not going to be easy. But there was another part of me that knew great opportunities were not just going to be handed to me. I had to go after what I wanted.

That's when I let the part of me that wanted my dream win over the part of me that was afraid. And through a series of events, I was led to the life mastery institute. I fell in love with their teachings. I enrolled in their program and went through their training process to become certified as a life coach. I attended long trainings and studied daily and discovered this proven, reliable system that turns dreams into reality. It's called the DreamBuilder system. It's based on 40 years of research, studying the most successful people and how they used ten success principles to turn their desires into reality. I applied those principles to my life, and everything changed!

Today, exactly one year after submitting my two-week notice, I am the most fulfilled I have ever been. I wake up with gratitude, feeling energetic and ready to take on the day. I am able to draw boundaries where they need to be drawn. I have the best relationship with my boys, and I get to enjoy all the quality time I desperately wanted with them. I get to do what I love, which is making a real difference in people's lives while still being able to work as a Respiratory Therapist. I love the extraordinary differences I have already made, and I'm looking forward to achieving my goal of touching 500 lives by September 18, 2023.

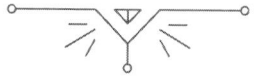

Does it Matter?

Tamara Angel Oswald
NEVADA, USA

Six years old, and I find myself being molested by an older man again. I am disgusted with myself for being in this situation. I do not know how to get away. I feel like I need to do what he wants, or he will do something even worse.

Seven years old, and I awake to my mom's upset voice; she is angry and scared because her new husband had just beaten her up so he could have her paycheck. As I walk out of the room, she looks at me through her swelled-up black eye with the phone to her ear. She says, "Your aunt will be here soon. Pack your things. We're moving." We move often, so I am used to it, but this time I must give away my dogs. On the other hand, I am glad that I do not have to see that old man again.

Seven years old, I walk into my run-down very dark apartment to see a man sitting on the couch. The coffee table is littered with marijuana, a spoon, syringe, lighter and a big rubber band. My mom comes into the room to find me looking at Andy, her boyfriend. She watches my eyes gaze toward the coffee table, then up to her. She looks at the scene and walks over to where Andy is sitting and says to get that stuff out of her house.

I'm nine years old, and Andy is still doing drugs and drinking. He is nice sometimes and other times he is explosive. His bushy, curly, hair and ragged beard make him look even scarier. He likes to humiliate me in front of friends and other adults.

Eleven years old, and we move to a new apartment. This one has a pool. I complete my chores and am excited to be able to go to the pool with my friends. I love spending time immersed under water where I can drown out the noise of the world. My only peace.

Coming up for air in the deep end, I see Andy standing at the entrance to the pool area. He looks angry. Putting his hand up he motions for me to follow him. I know I must, as he is the authority. We walk into the clean house that I am proud of, and he points to a napkin which is hidden behind a table. He takes off his belt and beats me with it. I am crying because it hurts, and I am ashamed, so I hide myself in my room.

I'm twelve years old, and my mom arrives home. I walk into the kitchen to see Andy's fist clinched back and the other full of my mom's hair; he is ready to punch her in the face. I scream at him to leave her alone. He turns and hits me so hard that he knocks me out.

I'm thirteen years old, and my friend and I are going to church. One of the church parishioners asks if we would like a ride home. We accept. We end up in his locked basement looking for a way out. We climb through a small window that is high above our heads. I stand on my friend's shoulders and climb through; I am standing at ground level so I reach to pull her through. We run home and tell her mom, who has the man arrested.

Age fifteen, and my mom has had enough of Andy's abuse and

splits up with him for good. Andy shoots himself in the head. My mom does not know how to express her emotions, so she buries herself in her work.

I am married. My mom moves in with us. Her presence brings up so much hurt. I resent her for putting me in all of these situations. I let myself become bogged down by all the years of unfairness. I wake up angry and I go to bed angry. I lack confidence and am full of shame that I just want to keep hidden. My anger is taking a toll on my marriage and relationships with my kids. My work performance is in the toilet. I feel like I cannot do anything right.

Is this all there is to life? Just to suffer and *die*? I see other people living happy lives. I know there is something I am missing. I decide to find out how to be happy. I love this quote.

"As a man thinketh in his heart so he is."
—PROVERBS 23:7

Since I asked, Spirit chose to show me there is a whole new way of thinking.

First, I learn we are all governed by the laws of the Universe and our results are a direct reflection of the way we think and speak about ourselves and others.

Second, the thing is the feeling of shame and anger are not from Spirit. Nothing is created without a few mistakes in the process. Grace is required. Knowing this gives me the confidence to take the steps to find my true purpose.

Creating a shift in my thought process helps me to understand that each one of us is working from current knowledge, but we have access to a whole lot more that changes our entire lives if we tap into it. All the things that happened before could have left me either captive, dead, or a drug addict, but instead I choose to say I was protected and loved through everything. Looking at it all from a positive perspective leaves me to appreciate the goodness that is always right in front of me.

Experimenting with my thoughts is a whole new way of living. Each day I tell myself these words: I am smart, funny, lovable, kind, worthy, and wise.

Finally, I have the power to think, believe, and speak the good things into my life, so I do. Now my life is completely different. I am full of confidence, love, and lots of wisdom. This shift in thinking has made my life so much better. My husband and I love spending time together now. He even took me to Hawaii, which was my 20-year dream. My kids and I are closer than ever. I even appreciate my mother for all the lessons she had to learn as well.

Being a life coach fills my heart, because helping others is my true passion. My free time is spent pouring love and joy out to everyone around me. Watching people feel loved and wanted fills me with joy.

So yes, it does matter. Everything happens for the greater good.

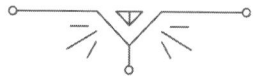

Waking Up to A New Reality

Trish Walker

UTAH, USA

I feel heavy, foreboding energy, on this otherwise sunny January morning. As usual, my mom left early in the morning for her shift as a nurse at the hospital. As I descend the stairs in my childhood home, back from college for a break, I call out to my dad, a pharmaceutical sales rep with flexible hours. However, the air feels uncharacteristically stagnant, and with every step I take, my gut tells me inevitable change is in the air.

I turn the corner into our family room, and that's when I see my dad lying on the floor face down. Panicked, I rush to him, turn him over, and try to find a pulse or other signs of life. Ironically, I had just learned basic CPR in my high school health class several months ago, which is why I knew immediately there was nothing I could do. His lifeless eyes meant just one thing; my precious dad was gone. Forever.

Evidently, he had been out shoveling snow, felt bad, and came in to lie down, only to have a massive heart attack and die suddenly. Even if I had been there when it happened, there was nothing I could've done.

"No, no, no! This can't be happening," I mutter to my myself. Dad was just talking to me the night before while I got ready to go out with friends. What were our last words to each other? My dad was not one for emotions or love until he was close to death. I'm now certain he had a feeling he was in the homestretch. We later find out that he had just turned in his forms for early retirement. He had also paid his bills early that month.

I run to the phone and dial 9-1-1. I feel out of my body for the next few hours while I call my siblings and sob into the phone. I'm the youngest of five kids and I'm the one who has to tell everyone. I make all of these calls before the slow-moving rescue squad arrives, after which the paramedics ask me all kinds of questions, making me feel like I did something wrong.

At some point, the police arrive to take me over to my brother's house. Walking to the squad car, I notice neighbors peeking through curtains, but they never come out. Thirty years later and I still remember their faces looking at me. Why don't you come out and help?

Recently I turned the age my dad was when he died. And you know what? I didn't die. Until now, I didn't realize I was holding onto some sort of "supposed curse" that I too would pass at that same age. Two days before this milestone birthday I suddenly got very emotional, and I let go of a lot of things, including how I felt the day I found my dad on the floor. In this moment of enlightenment, I see that over the years, I've always stopped myself from going big, because what's the point? I had this buried belief that I would just drop dead early in life the way my dad did.

Grief is its own entity. Some days I don't feel sadness at all, and other days it stares me in the face. Over the years since my dad passed, I've lost my mom, a good friend, and recently experienced the death of a friendship with someone who was very important to me. And I've come to realize that grief is precipitated by all kinds of events and comes not just from the death of loved ones, but also from things like the loss of a job, the end of relationships, and even losses that you bring on yourself (regardless of the reason). Grief is a part of life, not a projection of the future.

No one knows how we'll each handle our own grieving process. So rather than let the grief of my dad's death scare me, I now choose to honor my dad by living a big life, helping others going through similar journeys.

On my actual "death" birthday, I go for a long, meaningful hike by myself. During that time, I feel my dad's spirit all around me. I can tell he's with me, telling me I still have so much more to give to the world. I stop and whisper, "Dad, if you are listening, in some strange way, I'm honored you chose me to find you after you passed, because it's taught me some valuable lessons and I use them to help others."

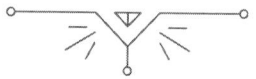

My Awakening

Cheetra Ramcharn
CANADA

I feel the cool breeze on my skin as I sit under a tree on the bank of the river. The sound of the water flowing is so relaxing. I hold on to the book I am reading, and as I raise my face to the sky, looking for an answer, I close my eyes to protect them from the sun shining through the foliage.

I hear the wheels squeaking as someone pushes the trolley towards the operation theatre. Fear grips me as I ask myself: What if I have an adverse reaction to the anesthesia? What if my body does not heal, and worst of all, how will I continue with my life after this surgery? I close my eyes against the morning sun streaming through the windows in the hospital corridor, and in my prayer, I implore my angels to stay by me and protect me through the procedure.

So many people bustling around, and a doctor pushes a needle into my hand; as I gasp with pain, I hear him say, "She is ready." No, I am still conscious, and I fear feeling the scalpel! A gentler voice asks me to breathe deeply and count to ten, and I remember counting to three. I wake up feeling both hot and cold and so nauseated. Every time I push away the blanket, somebody tucks me in. The first couple of days, responding to the pain medicine, I sleep most of the time. Then on the third day with no morphine, I plummet into the abyss of despair. I always wanted to have a baby. Now, I feel like a lesser woman, as my body will never carry a baby. I am in the hospital bed sobbing at my loss as I ask myself, "What did I do wrong to deserve this? Is it my karma again—my past life actions affecting my present?"

I hear voices coming closer, and as I open my eyes, two gentlemen are going by in a canoe. One of them says, "That's extremely smart of you, sitting in the shade and reading, not like us working hard in the sun!" Smart is the last thing I'm feeling right now. I re-read the paragraph in my book on the probable cause of fibroid tumors: nursing a hurt from a partner, a blow to the female ego.

Yes, that's what I do. I run the story over and over again in my mind. I re-live the arguments and harsh words for days after they happen! My thoughts created the fibroids by my constant rehashing of the past. I blame my negative pattern of thinking for the hysterectomy. I feel so guilty I want to scream; instead, I close my eyes, pretending to meditate as more people go by in canoes.

Up until now, those close to me have told me I have bad karma. Up until now, I have blamed my bad karma for my life circumstances. Fair skin equates to beauty in my culture, and I have very dark skin. An elementary school friend told me I was born dark as a punishment for something I did wrong in my past life—I somehow believe her. I must have done something awful to be punished like this. And as others make fun of me, I feel diminished and so lonely.

As I scan the pages of my book, I read more about how our thoughts create our reality, how a negative thought and emotion attract similar negative experiences. And I realize I've been wrong all along. It was not punishment for my past life's actions, but my current thoughts in this lifetime that created my life.

I now see how my beliefs of not being beautiful and worthy attract me to those who do not see me as worthy and are demeaning to me. It is so clear how I live in the victim cycle. My fear that others will make fun of me attracts to me those same experiences. My concern that people will criticize my skin color brings to me those who support those thoughts. Worst of all, my thoughts focusing on my hatred of my body and my dark skin bubble up too frequently. I feel terrible for being unkind to myself. I allow the shame and guilt to wash over me. I let the flowing water draw away all the negativity from my body. And I begin to feel differently.

The bubbling, flowing water feels peaceful. As I calm down, I hear this question: how can I change my thoughts to create a different life from now on? I feel so vulnerable. How can I even begin to do this? Where do I start? Do I have what it takes to change years of limiting thought patterns? I take a deep breath and say to myself it is now or never.

I am back at my favorite spot under the tree. I open my journal and start writing:

I am so grateful for a second chance in a new country.
I am so grateful to be alive and healthy.
I am learning to love my body.
I look in the mirror, and I like what I see.
It is all working out for me.
I am at peace.

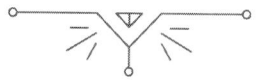

Dual Degrees

Suzanne M. Haney Oldridge

NEVADA, USA

It is almost midnight. I am lying in my bed under the orange, yellow, pink, and green paisley happy-looking bedspread. My hands are crossed on my chest and John Lennon's song "Imagine" is playing in the background while I wait. To die.

I am 16. I have been so unhappy for what feels like forever in my short life. I have been longing for something, although I am not sure what it is. I know that I will feel better when I find it. I will belong. I will be enough. I have searched for whatever it is in venues like smoking, drinking, drugs, and rebellion against parents and all authority in general. I have not found it, and I feel so bad; it is so dark no one can understand this pain. I am sad, scared, frustrated, and angry almost all the time.

I see no way out other than to leave this earth in a very loud way. My heart will explode by means of what I have done. This way, they will know how much pain I was in.

I lie there waiting, thinking there will be peace soon; the longing, pain and anguish will be gone.

And then it starts to happen. My heartbeat quickens. I can hear it in my ears as I feel it in my chest.

I am ready for this, I tell myself. All of this pain and darkness will be gone soon. I try to focus on the lyrics, "Imagine all the people, living life in peace . . ."

I am sweating now. My heart is racing so fast in my chest and booming so loudly in my ears that I can barely hear the music, and then I hear *it* . . ."You are not done here yet." What? Then, all of a sudden, I know. The voice is right! I am not done here. I do not want to die. Massive fear takes hold of me as I throw off the covers and run to my parents' room, just 20 feet away. I shake my dad to wake him up. "What, what—" he shouts as he startles awake, "—what's wrong?"

Through streaming tears, I tell him what I've done, and I am so scared now. I hear myself saying, "I don't want to die! I don't want to die!" He is up in a flash, pulling on his clothes as fast as he can. He knows he must get me to the hospital soon.

My mom is awake now and scared, wringing her hands, not knowing what to do, what to offer or what to say.

I see calm and concern in my dad's eyes. Fear is there too. I feel so bad now for the pain I've caused, and I want to live; I want to feel bad, to feel anything. I just want to live. I am so scared now that I know I want to live and that it may be too late. I start to freak out. My dad tells me to stay calm, that we will be at the hospital soon and it will be okay.

He is now concerned for my mom as well; she is worried, clasping and unclasping her hands, with nothing to do but wish this was not happening. My dad tells her to stay home while he takes me. If it does not work out, he wants to spare my mom from witnessing it.

We go quickly out to the car. My mom follows, watching us from the door with tears in her eyes as we get in the car and leave.

In my pajamas, the seat in the car feels cold. The five-minute drive to the hospital is quiet, unlike other times I've pushed limits. I feel pain in my body, in my mind, and in my heart. Through the pain, I know, and I am glad I chose to listen to that voice telling me that I was not done here yet.

That night I earned my first Dual Degree in failure and success. I failed at suicide and succeeded in living.

The voice was right. I was not done here.

I have had the privilege to continue living. I have acquired many more degrees in failure and success, including being a good daughter, wife, mother, friend, and athlete, in confidence, career, kindness, patience, loving, generosity, responsibility, and so many more.

I am so happy that I chose to listen to that still small voice that night, and I continue to listen and hear it today.

I am proud of my many dual degrees. They are life itself emerging and expressing itself through me and helping me to evolve so I can become the best version of myself in this life. I am so grateful to be still living.

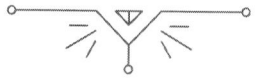

Finding Love
on the Fourth Date

Linda Lee Smith

SOUTH CAROLINA, USA

The dating agency said I was to dress to impress. So, here I am in a fancy restaurant, hair and nails done, dressed in my best colorful outfit—ready to impress! Will number four be better than the last three dates? I can only hope. He is brought to my table and as I look up, I think, "Hmmm, not bad a step up from the previous old men the agency promised were good matches for me."

He introduces himself as Rich. Grey hair, mustache, very tall and appears to be in great shape. But who am I to judge? Having spent 27 years in the convent, followed by 25 years creating educational programs that kept me busy traveling internationally—I have little to no experience with men, much less with dating. I'm in my seventies and just semi-retired from teaching. So, I'm just now wondering what it would be like to have a companion to go out to dinner with, to the theater or to a movie.

I like him and we find that we have a lot in common. I invite him to come back to my place after dinner to "see my Christmas tree!" Having just moved to Florida, I am feeling rather proud of myself for putting up Christmas decorations when it is 80 degrees outside!

We agree to have a second date, then a third, and now we are seeing each other just about every day. This is fun, but I'm sensing an underground panic beginning to develop within me. This could get serious I think; I can't play around with someone's life. I sit him down and tell him how I feel, that "I like him a lot, but more like a brother." To me, this seems like a nice thing to say, meaning "It's okay to hang out together, but let's not get too serious." He is visibly crushed, and then I feel bad for saying what I did. As an afterthought, I ask if he would like to come over for New Year's Eve and we could throw some steaks on the grill. My great inexperience in this "dating scene" is beginning to get me in trouble.

After some discussion, we agree to be companions, which relieves my panic. I just ask that he never bring up the "M" word. I cannot even say the word "marriage." It's hard for me at my age to admit I don't even know how companionship works. I just know that I love being with him. We walk the beach, enjoy sunsets, and hang out just about every day. We both love to cook, so we are zigging and zagging in the kitchen, enjoying our creations together.

I don't dare tell my good friends about Rich. I can already hear their questions. "What if this doesn't last?" "What if he tires of you?" "What if you get cold feet?" But then something happens. I win an all-expense paid leadership cruise for two including airfare! I wonder, should I take one of my girlfriends? But I would miss Rich. Dare I take him?

I don't hesitate. I ask him and he says yes. "You do know those cruise cabins only have one bed and a small bathroom," he cautions.

"I know, so maybe we ought to do a dry run?" I voice. He makes arrangements for a B&B in a coastal city not far away, and we have a successful weekend of fun. Things are going well. As for the cruise, many of my girlfriends are also on that cruise ship. No hiding Rich now! I receive lots of affirmations that I've chosen well.

We go zip lining, cave tubing, and explore several islands. Each time the ship docks, we go through the marketplaces, and curiously, I find myself strangely attracted to the jewelry shops. I'm exploring the diamond sections. I've been on many cruises, but this was the first time I ever noticed diamonds.

By March, Rich is moving in, and I make space for him not only in my home but in my heart as well. At the end of April, I will be going to Australia for six weeks to teach my last scheduled courses. Since Rich lives in my home now, I leave him several tasks to take care of in my absence and I give him a stack of business cards he just might need to refer to while I am gone. Somehow, a business card for a personal jeweler friend of mine managed to get in the stack. I'm not sure if that is a conscious move on my part or not.

It is a *long* six weeks to be away from him, made easier by our Skyping every single day. I awaken at 6:30 AM each day, get my cup of tea, and wait for his Skype to come through. It is the evening for him, and he tells me how his day went, and I tell him what I will be doing that day. These morning calls are what sealed my heart for him.

I return a few days before my birthday, and Rich tells me he plans a celebration at the very restaurant where we first met. Arriving, I see six beautiful red roses on the table. However, my thought jumps to, "There better be more than roses! I am ready for more in life."

At the end of the meal, he gets down on one knee and proposes, presenting me with a beautifully unique diamond ring as a token of his love. My heart jumps for joy. I have found the love of my life. I thank God that I didn't give up after those first three dates that didn't come anywhere near being a vibrational match for me. He was waiting for me as number four. Six months later, I am happily married for the very first time.

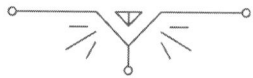

Blessed Twice

Richard Louis Schmelke
SOUTH CAROLINA, USA

My heart still aches. I still have episodes of spontaneous sobbing, and I am focusing on taking it one day at a time and putting one foot in front of the other to get through my day.

It has been a year since the loss of my beloved wife of forty years. Today is not too bad a day. I am sitting on my sofa in the living room, not thinking about much of anything, when a path appears before me. I am stunned, and it takes me a moment or two to gather myself. I see what seems to be two signs at the end of the path. I see myself getting off the sofa and walking toward the signs. I see that one sign points to the left. I look in that direction, and what I see is a life like the one I have been living—more grief, anger, bitterness, sadness, and loneliness. I turn to read the other sign. There is only one word on it, LIFE. I have no idea where it will lead me, but I instinctively choose that direction.

However, there is something else I must do, and I return to the sofa. I look up and an image of a shelf appears on the wall, and on that shelf are two extraordinarily large leather-bound books. Somehow, I know to select the one on the left. I open it. It contains every memory of the forty-three-year relationship I had with the fantastic woman who no longer shared my life. I turn to the last page and write THE END in bold letters. Something tells me I need to put the book back on the shelf. I take the other book down. It is full of empty pages. I turn to the first page and write, CHAPTER ONE OF MY NEW LIFE.

It has been several days since the experience of seeing the path. I notice that I am feeling a loneliness I have never experienced up until then. I have a deep longing for female companionship. I long for someone with whom to share my new life. Someone to go to a movie with or to walk on the beach alongside. Someone's hand to hold. For the first time in over a year, I begin to imagine what it would be like to have someone new in my life. I sit down and consider what kind of person I want as a companion. I have no idea how to find such a person, so I set that thought aside. A week later, I am sitting at my computer reading an ad for a vetted dating agency. Something inside of me tells me to answer the ad. And I do.

It is mid-December, and I am having dinner with a woman I met through the agency. There is something exceptional about her. We begin to date and have fun together. Sometime around late March or early April, I am taking a massive step in our relationship. I am buying a diamond ring. Linda is in Australia teaching, and we are Skyping every day. It's early morning for her and just past suppertime for me. We are like two starry-eyed teenagers when we talk to each other. I'm falling more and more in love with her. I am eagerly anticipating her return. It's June 6th, Linda's birthday, and we are at the restaurant where we met. I have the engagement ring in my pocket and am trying to find the perfect time to propose. When I can no longer stand the suspense, I muster the courage, go to her side of the table, get on my knee, and propose. I am thrilled when she says yes.

In the days and months that follow, the trajectory of my life takes a turn after I attend a couple of conferences as Linda's guest. Then, finally, I hear the message that it is okay to want something more out of life and that it wasn't selfish to want the happiness I once enjoyed.

Linda and I are married on December 16, 2017. I am truly blessed to have found deep, profound love and joy, not once but twice in my life.

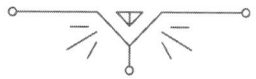

Healing for Life

Janice Marie Long
MARYLAND, USA

Shining my light feels easy as a young, carefree athlete. Life is cool and the future exciting. Halfway through my 18th year, on the 29th of June, my brother chooses to end his life. Deep inner fear and anxiety grow inside of me in the massive void that remains. Decisions made by this once fearless, joyful spirit, as I search for support and love during this devastating time, take me down a darker path.

My parents split after 31 years. My older sister and brother are both married. The loneliness is unbearable. It is difficult to know what to say during these trying times, but people feel compelled to say something. At a party, picnic, or bonfire, when I can finally think of something else for a few moments, there it is, "I'm sorry about your brother." Wham, gutted, time after time. Lost, I accept a date with a guy I turned down before my brother's death. He is eight years older, and I find the conversation more stimulating than with boys my age. I am unaware of how in-over-my-head I am.

Pregnant in my junior year of college, we secretly marry on my spring break in the Florida Keys. I optimistically accept this unexpected role of wife and motherhood. Two boys, two girls, and a house in the 'burbs. I love my family and smile publicly, yet privately my heart tells a different story. The emotional stress of just surviving a loveless marriage takes its toll. Low vibrational frequencies trapped in my energy field cause dysfunction and disease in my body. Migraines, TMJ, three cervical spine herniations, chronic fatigue, psoriasis, anxiety, depression, and inexplicable back pain wreak havoc within me. It is the breast cancer diagnosis that finally gives me the courage to choose life, a life I love living. On my journey, I learn so many beautiful healing methods illuminating a new path for myself and others. Not only is there a way out of pain, but we are also not alone.

Joanne's eyes welled with tears as she shared her dream. "I would love to play the piano again." My body radiates with chills, a reaction I recognize as communication from the divine source. "I could make the piano cry. So mystical and so beautiful. It took me a year to prepare those five pages of music. I'm so thankful to God for the opportunity to play for my father one last time, but it's been 16 years."

She is a kind and passionate kindergarten teacher bringing out the best in every child entrusted to her care. I teach her a movement therapy, the Feldenkrais Method, to supplement her ongoing intensive physical therapy. Her susceptibility to debilitating injury, from seemingly nothing, is a mystery to doctors. A child pulls on her arm to get her attention, and it may take a month or several to recover. Picking up a chair to move it disables her for weeks. A mysterious burning in her neck is severe when she attempts to play piano. Her life feels very limited. While she accepts where she is, the sadness and frustration are there.

I shyly tell her about the energy clearing I have been studying that is healing my body and changing my life in ways I never believed were possible. I worry about rejection as the words flow past my lips. I know she has a strong religious background and feel unsure of how my offering will be received.

We begin a journey through the Emotion Code and Body Code that hold the keys to releasing trapped emotions to allow the healing of the deep wounds of the past. Her increased physical stamina and ability to partake in simple and more complex activities is life-changing for her. Two beautiful piano recordings arrive by text. They are breathtaking. A few months later she told me the heartfelt gratitude she feels to have been able to play for her mother while here on earth and again at her final farewell.

Dean walks into the studio the way most strangers off the street do, asking what we offer and how much we charge. "We are different than a gym," I begin. Abruptly, he gasps and grapples for his legs. What is happening? His difficulty standing is pain shooting through a body that has endured three back surgeries, the second to insert a rod along his spine, the third to remove, shorten and reinsert the rod. He is close to retirement. Movement is excruciating. Life is hard. The pain is overtaking his existence. We proceed with care. Getting up and down onto the table or reformer is exhausting for him. It is difficult to watch, especially as an empath. As the trust builds between us, his body begins the process of rewiring. I am guided to share a deeper level of healing. As a previous non-believer in energy work, the fear of rejection, up until now, has been an invisible barrier to sharing this powerful work.

He allows me to ask questions to his subconscious on his behalf. A psychic trauma is where two emotions are trapped simultaneously and need to be released together. Horror and grief from age 20. He was a college student and had just received news that his two best friends were killed in the same week in Vietnam. We cried together. This is a new beginning to his healing journey.

Our appointments are more spaced out now. He does his homework—sketches I write up to support him since he is now living forty-five minutes away. He now moves with ease into the studio, not the shadow of himself he once was, but standing tall and beaming from ear to ear. He sits back on the table, waiting patiently for me to finish with the client before him.

I walk toward him wearing a curious smirk. He jumps to his feet, hands on hips and smile gleaming. "Ready?" I nod. He bends down, slaps the floor with both hands and pops back up, three times in rapid fire! He radiates strength, happiness, and a love for life.

"Thank you for saving me from becoming the grouchy old man, shaking an umbrella over his head and mad at the world." He hands me a note. "This is from my wife." Inside it reads, "Thank you for giving me back my boyfriend, Lynne."

I am a spiritual being having a human experience. I understand everything is energy. Energy and frequency are the keys to healing. I am so grateful for my vibrant health, the courage to speak truth without fear of rejection, and especially shining bright and sharing my light for others.

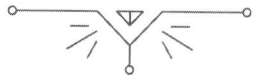

Grief Awakens

Hanna Gorecka
CANADA

My dad holds my tiny hand as we walk into the lush green foliage of the forest. I feel the warm sunshine on my face—I am enjoying a beautiful day in Poland. I am inhaling the scent of the forest and I have a sense of safety and deep calm. Dad points to the abundance of blueberries on the bed of bushes, and we start collecting them into our wicker baskets. I say "Dad, look at the size of these!" The sweet flavor bursts when I bite into them. Dad takes out his camera from a bag with an arsenal of photographic equipment and proceeds to capture endless images. I observe him in a mindful moment of artistic passion. Time disappears and we become deeply connected with nature.

In the evening Dad leads the way to his photography studio and the dark room. The small space is saturated with an intense scent of chemicals. With excitement, he proceeds to involve me in the development of photos he captured earlier that day. "Can I help you with the processing, Dad?" We gently shuffle blank pieces of photo paper in the solution as we watch black and white images slowly unveil themselves. Dad hangs the photos with clips on metal strings as one would with freshly washed laundry. I am intrigued and enamored by this magical process. "Dad, being with you is always an adventure!"

In the late 1980s, my parents are forced to escape Poland due to a communist regime and difficult life, with three kids and one suitcase each. They leave successful careers, family, friends, and our entire support system behind and move to Canada in search of greener pastures. I am 11 years old, uprooted from my entire world, but with time I assimilate and find a new way. My dad, an engineer, is pursuing a new education and a physically draining job to support the household. He is working full-time and taking six courses per semester at NAIT. He barely sleeps, never calls in sick—all this without proper knowledge of the English language. He pushes through each day and shows us kids incredible resilience and dedication in times of adversity. Finally, at the age of 70, Dad announces that he is retiring and is excited about pursuing long-neglected hobbies.

One Monday in December I have an unusual feeling that I need to see my parents. We schedule an out-of-routine midday walk in our area. Dad arrives and emerges from the car with a radiant and contagious smile, and offers a joke to further brighten our day. He is in a great mood and full of life. He says "I am doing 80 push-ups daily, I am running up and down the stairs, I am exploding with energy, and I will live until 100 years at least!" We all laugh. My dad captures a photo of my six-year-old son and me with a snowman that we randomly come upon on our path. After the sunny walk is over, my son asks my dad to check out a snow fort he built by our front door, but Dad is in a hurry and insists he'll see the snow structure when he returns for a visit on the weekend. We warmly hug and say goodbye.

It is Thursday evening. I am getting my son ready for a ski lesson when the phone rings; it is my brother, and he asks me "Are you sitting down, Sis?" I sit down. "What is happening, Greg?" I ask with apprehension. My brother proceeds to tell me that Dad has had a stroke. I cannot comprehend what my brother is saying as I sit frozen in shock. Four days later my dad takes his last breath by my side and crosses over right after I say a heartfelt farewell. His departure completely shatters my life and that of everyone who loved him. Life can change in an instant, but I never thought it would happen so early, just a year after his retirement. "How do I go on without my dad?" I ask myself, "Without my foundation and support?"

This profound loss changes my sense of identity and the course of my life. Life wakes me up to feeling immense grief. When the waves of grief hit me, it is debilitating. In search of solace, I read multiple books on bereavement, and I learn that once I move through grief, the world will feel brighter, the sense of beauty and gratitude will be enhanced. I surrender to the suffering and embrace the feelings in order to heal. I understand that I have to create time for stillness in order to embark on a path to a trans-formed self. The passing of time, being with family, and spending time in nature allows me to move forward toward the sense of unity. When I can do little for myself, when I feel disconnected and devastated, my son and my husband hold me, my friends bring me delicious meals and listen. Every act of kindness reminds me that I am loved, even when I am at my lowest. It is the community that nourishes, accepts, and carries me. If it was not for the web of people around me, I would have perished.

Today, I am holding my young son's hand as we enter the for-est. We take a deep breath, immersing ourselves in the smells and sounds of nature as we listen to and watch the water flowing down the creek. We listen to various birds chirping and leaves gently fluttering in the wind. We pause and engage all of our senses, take photos, talk about Grandpa, and share special memories. "Look Mom, here is the spot where Grandpa took the last picture of us!" We bottle up the special sense of that day; the sunshine, great conversation and humor. We find Dad in every fragment of nature. In the cycle of life—a life ends, and another begins and has an opportunity to continue the legacy, to make this world a connected and meaningful place.

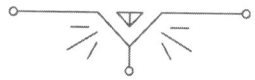

Fly Home

Jenn MacMullin
CANADA

I am standing at the kitchen sink washing the dishes; the sunlight is streaming in, filling the kitchen with light. I turn to see my husband walking in, looking at me.

"I got the transfer; we are going to Alberta," he says, looking pleased. We have been on this military base for three years now, in our home province of Nova Scotia. We've been waiting months to hear this news.

I feel apprehensive. I hoped for a base in British Columbia. I can see myself there, not in Alberta. I have been feeling isolated and anxious and feel our marriage has gotten to a breaking point.

Do I have to go? Should I go? I don't feel heard, or that I have a say in anything in our marriage or our finances. I don't see the bills. My husband is either working or tucked away in the spare room on his computer. We don't talk. I am starting to feel like a piece of luggage to be taken to Alberta, not a wife going on an adventure.

Would a change of location and job help us? Do I believe this? No, but I am willing to try. He is my husband. I will have to end my community health and wellness newsletter I started almost a year ago, and my volunteer work, and move across the country.

Three months have passed and my husband and I are settled into our military base house in Alberta. I am doing all I can to make it feel like a home. I am loving my new job as a Chiropractic Assistant, connecting with the patients and listening to their stories.

The weeks are flying by. It's been a long day, and driving home, I walk through the door to our home. The entrance is tight, and the house is dark and cold. I feel a tightness in my chest. I can't breathe. I am struggling to take my coat off. I don't want to be here in this house with my husband. I head straight up the stairs to our bedroom. My husband is in the spare room on his computer; it's late and I am anxious. He spends every evening there. He doesn't talk to me, but he appears to be enjoying talking to other people late into the night.

I am sitting upright in bed, awakened by a voice, a very loud voice saying, "leave." I look around for the voice in the dark, sitting straight up. Where is the voice coming from? It was just a dream, but I heard a voice. I look to my right; my husband is asleep beside me. It is the middle of the night. I can't leave now. I keep my eyes on the bedroom window, watching the morning sunlight come in.

It is 5:30 AM, and I am putting on my sweats and tying up my sneakers. I jump into the passenger side of our car, and my husband gets into the driver's side. We drive across the military gate; my husband gets out of the car at his work, and the door slams shut.

I am feeling nervous, and anxiously remember the voice that woke me up earlier. I drive home by myself, walk up to the entrance, and close the door. The house is still, but I feel panic. Again, I can't breathe. I look at the clock, and it's 6:00 AM. I pick up the phone and dial, and Mom answers. "I need to leave right now," I tell her. I hang up the phone and begin running through the house. I look through each bookshelf, cupboard, and closet. What do I take? I am not prepared; I should have packed a suitcase a while ago. I knew I would have to leave. The question was when. I quickly pull out my clothes, photos, and books and load them into our car.

I feel like a thief in the night. I am fearful that my husband or the military police will show up any minute and catch me leaving. I must get to work by 9:00 AM. How am I going to do that? I am leaving my husband. I look at the inside of the small, four-door car. Everything is jammed into it. I keep looking at the neighbor's house. Is anyone coming?

I lock the house and drive to the office; I walk through until I see my boss. "I have left my husband." I see the shock cross his face. "You can work it out," he tells me. I tell him I can't be here when my husband gets off work and comes looking for me and the car.

I see my boss's wife walk toward us and I feel a sigh of relief. She will work for me today. I pick up the phone and call the police. "I left my husband and didn't leave a note." I had not left a note to a man who would not talk to me. We didn't discuss things or make decisions together. I have not felt safe having a conversation about leaving. During our marriage, I've lost my voice, control of my life, and who I am. I have anxiety and have gained a lot of weight. "I will call your husband," I hear the officer say. "Here's the number to the women's shelter."

I recall the quote I love by Ralph Waldo Emerson. "Once you make a decision, the universe conspires to make it happen."

Nearly three weeks have passed, and everything is falling into place. I am a woman on a mission, staying at the women's shelter. I have all my belongings on a moving truck, and I have hired and trained someone to take my job. I have a plane ticket, a bus booked to take me to the airport, and a lawyer.

I am relieved that I listened to my still small voice, my inner knowing. I trusted myself that this marriage did not feel right. I did not know how I was going to leave, or where I was going to stay, but I took the actions needed to get myself out, and everything fell into place.

As I fly home to Nova Scotia, looking at the clouds, I feel the strength and peacefulness within me that was always there. I am going to heal and create a life I love!

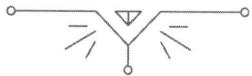

They Ought to Do Something

Dawn Zehren
WISCONSIN, USA

"They ought to name the theatre after him," is my first thought as I hear that Mr. Hidde will retire at the end of the school year.

Dale K. Hidde taught speech and theatre arts at Wauwatosa East High School, locally referred to as "Tosa East." It seemed like Dale lived at the theatre, spending his nights and weekends working on projects. He poured himself into his craft. The results showed. His theatre program earned the name "The Award-Winning Tosa East Players." That title was only a reflection of his legacy. He created extraordinary shows by developing the skills and character of thousands of students. His standards required students to stretch and grow. Each student could be seen and heard. Working together, they would shine.

I remember going to my first Players meeting at the start of freshman year. I knew that was where I wanted to be.

The first show was so exciting. Opening night, walking towards the audience, I stepped out of my shoe. I was a newbie, but I knew better than to turn around and retrieve it. Instead, I hit my marks, took my bow, and grinned from ear to ear.

The next show was a drama with a small cast. That's when I became a Techie. Wherever I was needed—that is where I wanted to be. Over four years, I learned and did almost everything from sweeping the stage to calling the cues.

Dale taught me the value of vision, teamwork, persistence, listening, patience, and humility. He taught me how to lead myself and others.

Players became my second family, and that stage was my second home.

Now hearing that Dale is going to retire, a flurry of questions storms my mind: "What is he going to do next? How many students' lives did he change? What are they going to do to honor him? How can I honor him?"

While only 11 years out of high school, I know that in my lifetime there is no way I can repay him for everything I gained as a Tosa East Player.

If I cannot repay him, I could certainly thank him. But how?

My mind reels. "I can get some past grads together for a dinner or a luncheon. Hmm. We'd have to go to a restaurant. None of us have homes that would fit more than a few people." I am making up stories that gathering 20 people might be hard to pull off, but I really don't believe that. After all, Dale taught me how to produce events.

Quickly, grander thoughts come to mind: "What if I could host a reunion of Players spanning all the years that he taught?" Just as quickly, I am discouraged by thoughts of why I can't do it.

Back and forth I go. For every exciting idea I want to make real, I think of reasons why I can't. "I don't have the space, the money, the time, the connections." This is getting to be too much. I distract myself and drown out the ideas. Or so I think.

Over the next few days, it seems everyone I talk to wants to know, "What are *they* going to do to honor Mr. Hidde?" The funny thing is nobody seems to know who *they* are.

Then one night, my dad echoes my very first thought. "They ought to name the theatre after him." When I hear my dad say it, I know who *they* are. I'm sure I always knew; I just didn't want to admit it. I am *they*. I believe the theatre should be named after him. It is my work to do.

Dang, it! I still don't know how.

Nothing about this feels easy. It is not convenient, and I am scared. I'm worried that I don't have what it takes. I worry that if I try and fail, it will be a big public failure.

Driving home from my folks' house, alone with my thoughts, I find clarity. This isn't about me. This is for my mentor, whom I have come to call my friend. I want to honor him and show him the impact he made. I may not succeed, but I know that if I don't try, I will regret it. I decide; I am doing this.

My first move is to take away any chance to back out. I tell my two closest friends from Players what I aim to do. I admit I don't know how, and I ask for their help. Of course, they jump in. I tell a few more people. They join in too. Stacking the deck in my favor, I gain momentum and confidence.

It's time to tell Dale some of the plans. I ask to use the stage to host his retirement party, a grand reunion. While we need his help to compile the guest list, the team will do the work. He has no idea we are working to name the theatre after him.

A team of alumni, current students, and parents band together for a common goal. Our standards are high. Each person shares their ideas and resources. We stretch past our comfort zones, learn new skills, meet new people, take risks, fail, and try again and again. Together, we shine our light.

The big night arrives, and I am amazed. Past grads spanning 33 years have traveled to Wisconsin from California, Texas, New York, and states in between. Over 180 people gather to reminisce, share stories and celebrate. This isn't a class reunion; it is a family reunion honoring the man who, without ever being a parent, helped raise up so many teens.

Watching Dale light up as each person comes to thank him, my heart is full. I am so glad I did not give in to fear just because I didn't know how to make this happen. It is a full-circle moment. After all, each time I said yes to being in a show, or took on a new tech role, I didn't know how to do it. I just knew it was mine to do and kept taking the next step. It is exactly what Dale taught me.

And here we are, celebrating him, his legacy, and the space he created—The Dale K. Hidde Theatre.

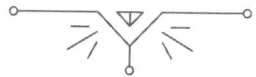

Butterfly Wings

Lydia Ruth Regier

PENNSYLVANIA, USA

One of my new teacher friends yells from the hallway communal phone, "Lydia, the phone is for you!" It is summer, and my first day of a teacher training program. I am spending three weeks in a boarding school with the rest of the teachers in training. I run down the hall. On the other end of the phone is my husband, who tells me the school where I interviewed a couple of weeks ago called. I hang up with him and I immediately call the school. The school's founder says they want to hire me as their fourth grade teacher. They want to know, if I am hired, will I continue to teach the children until they graduate from the eighth grade? I say, "Yes!" Then the lady says, "The parents have only one question, 'Will you *love* the children?'"

I begin teaching that fall in the fourth grade classroom. I think about how I always wanted to be a teacher, and I am excited to have my very own class. I think of all the work I did to get here. This is truly my dream come true! I do not have any children of my own, and I cherish the days watching these beautiful students grow and learn. I feel honored to be such an important part of their lives, and I *do love* the children! I also love lesson planning, studying the school's philosophy, and working with the parents. I follow the students through their fourth, fifth and sixth grade years.

In the middle of my students' seventh grade year, my mother becomes terminally ill with pancreatic cancer. My mother and I are extremely close and I am her only child. I realize that time is very short, and there are so many things I want to do with my mother and so many things I want to say to her. I want to quit my job and just be with her, but she wants to act like things are normal, like she's not sick. She keeps working as much as she can, and she wants me to keep doing what I love—teaching—because she knows that I love the children. I continue teaching and visiting my mother when she needs me. Within four months, she is gone. I am devastated.

A few months pass. My students are in eighth grade now. I am really proud of them! They will graduate this year and move on to high schools of their choice. My heart is aching, though. I love my students, but I miss my mom. She would want me to continue teaching because that is what makes me happy. I sense the governing body of the school is concerned about my teaching ability after such a loss. However, I know I am performing my best teaching lessons ever, although nobody is taking notice. I feel my best when I am teaching the students, but on breaks, grief hits me like a tidal wave. I request a schedule change. It is denied. Next, I ask for a short leave of absence. The answer to my request is, "No. We feel it would be best if you just stay home and heal." My mouth is dropping. I do not know what to say. Do they mean permanently? Yes, they think that is best. I can tell it would be futile to try to change their minds. I ask to come to school one more day to say good-bye to the children I love so dearly with all my heart.

The children are shocked as they walk into the classroom. With tears in my eyes, I tell them that we do not have to like the school's decision, but we have to respect it. I tell them that out of all the lessons I have taught them, my last lesson for them today is the most important one: sometimes we cannot choose what happens to us, but we can choose how we respond.

"Great lesson," I am thinking, "but now, how do I respond?" I am not only grieving the loss of my mother, but I've also lost my job, my career, my calling and my income! I can't believe I won't be able to teach my lovely children again or experience the camaraderie of the staff and parents. I feel like I've lost my purpose. I am alone and I don't know what to do. I thought I worked with compassionate people. How can they not understand my grief? What am I going to do now? Should I teach somewhere else? Do I even want to teach again? I don't know any of these answers. All I know is that I feel cheated.

My husband and I move back into my childhood home. It is bittersweet. I give myself space and time to grow and to rediscover who I am. Do I dare spread my crumpled wings? They feel so delicate and strange. I eventually allow myself to feel hope and happiness through the darkness. A little flicker of light appears in my heart as I notice my core truth and values have not changed. Underneath all of this pain and grief, could there possibly be a teacher who wants to fly again? Yes! I still have a passion for education and a calling to teach. However, this time, I plan to teach differently. I trust my wings again and form my own business, tutoring children. In a couple of years, I have a son and I begin homeschooling him when he is of age.

A few years later, I yearn to expand my business and to improve my whole life. A life coach helps me build that dream.

She understands. She encourages me to keep listening to my voice inside, my truth. My coach reminds me to take the step I can take today and to ask myself, "What can I do now with what I have, from where I am?" Answering that question, I step into my greater purpose. I become a life coach. Guiding others to follow their dreams, I discover I am unlocking my own. I am spreading my wings once more. I give thanks to the struggles, and I am grateful for my butterfly wings.

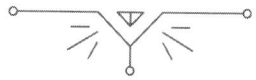

He is Not Here

Lois Leonard
CANADA

"Happy Birthday, Sis! Love Doug. PS Drat! Foiled again." Looking from the card to the present wrapped in tinfoil, I chuckle. He has a way of making me laugh and smile with his quick, wordplay humor. One of many precious and treasured memories that will flood my mind today. I will need them all.

Sitting in the second row of the chapel with my hands clenched and heart pounding, I am attempting to not completely fall apart. The sound of his favorite piano melody is playing in the background. My cheeks feel wet as I notice the tears start to flow. I wipe them away, trying to stop them without success. This cannot be real. We were supposed to grow old together. The mahogany casket sitting center stage is a focus point.

Beautiful craftsmanship. The carpenter in him would approve. I know this in my heart. This is not how I want to remember him. In a box. He is not there.

He is steadying the big blue two-wheeler holding the handlebars and back of the seat. I try to balance as I get ready to go. I am excited. I had pestered him to teach me how to ride. "I am old enough to learn. Please, please, please teach me how!"

"Ready?" he asks. I nod. Do I dare tell him how scared I am? He pushes and then he lets go. I glance down at my feet and hear him yelling at me. I look up just as I ride over the wall between our yard from the neighbor's. The bike is a little bent and I am a little shaken up and humiliated, but not hurt. I stand up to hear him say, "Great start, next time try to stay on the driveway, it works better. Just because the first time was not perfect, look at it as a first step taken, and keep trying, if you want it."

The patience and care he had for family, friends, and strangers was a gift. I was one of the luckiest benefactors of that gift.

Friends and family are entering the chapel to come to pay their respects and say goodbye. This is becoming real. I glance at the casket. My eyes start to leak, again. I do not want to say goodbye. He is not there.

He is standing in the row behind me, his hand on my shoulder. It is confirmation day at the local Catholic Church, and he is my sponsor to becoming an "adult." Neither the church nor my father was happy for my 17-year old brother to be my sponsor, as he was not considered an adult nor was he a female. I told them that if he could not be my sponsor, there was no one else I wanted to fulfill the role; they could count me out. As I had decided for him, he decided for me. This is the moment I learned to stand up for my beliefs, even when others did not.

I hear the sound of murmured conversation and a feeling of sadness filling the space. I am back in the second row. My family is sitting in front of me and around me. I cannot escape. Stop! How can I stall this nightmare or go back in time to stop it? My eyes scan the room and rest upon the casket again. He is not there.

He is accompanying me, arm-in-arm, down the aisle. He is in a black tuxedo, and I am in a white satin dress with pearls. It is my wedding day. Family and friends have come from miles away to celebrate with us on our happy day. I am so ecstatic. We arrive at the altar, and he puts my hand in the groom's and whispers, "I love you, I am so proud of you, and I will always be here for you."

This is true. He has always been there, showing and teaching me things when I was not paying attention. If I had been, I probably would have argued with him.

At sixteen, I believed fully I was getting my driver's license just because I was sixteen and wanted it. He declared that I would have to learn all about cars, changing the oil, and rotating the tires before I could learn to drive. "It is a privilege, not a right," he said. My parents agreed. I was so angry. I wanted my driver's license more than anything else. Every time I change a tire or check the oil, I thank him for standing his ground.

His spirit was expansive with love. With compassion, creating an awareness in my father for a better way to respond to a child's success in a school subject's exam is not to ask what they got wrong but to celebrate what they accomplished. The time to review was later.

A voice brings me back, declaring how troubling it is that his life had been cut short so young. He had so much more to give. The pain inside engulfs me. Dear God, please stop this. I am not ready to say goodbye. The voice is right, as more tears slip down my cheek and I begin to sniffle. My brother was young with a lot more to give. Gazing at the casket and the individuals, all I want . . . is for him to be here. I miss him.

But he is not there.

He is holding my two-week-old daughter as she clutches his

shirt and looks up at him. He has a smile on his face and love in his eyes. It's a memory to last a lifetime. I snap the picture, and, in my mind, I see him teaching her all the things he taught me.

But he is not here.

It is three months later. I am sitting in the second row in a chapel, having to say goodbye to the gentle giant of a man who meant the world to me.

A voice whispers, "The view is great from where I am. I get to watch over you all the time. Teach her the things I have taught you. I love you and I am so proud of you. I will always be here for you. You will be okay."

With a smile and warmth moving through me, I look back at the beautiful mahogany box at center stage. I know he is not there.

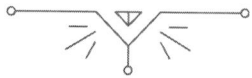

Power of Vision

Sigrid Igland
NORWAY

I'm 11 years old, sitting near the back of my fifth-grade classroom in Norway. The English teacher, a tall, elderly man with a loud voice says, "Sigrid, can you please share about the text you had for homework?" I look at all the other boys and girls, so many of them with their hands straight up, eager to be chosen. Why does he always choose me? I didn't even put my hand up.

My mind goes blank. I freeze. My heart starts beating loudly inside, and I give a short prayer that the lecture will be over soon. I am so afraid and embarrassed—I want to be sucked into the floor to never return.

Even during the summer holiday the lectures in English are still haunting me. Wow, today is actually a Wednesday and there is no lecture in English! I feel relieved and grateful.

A couple of years later, I find myself in secondary school. The new English teacher is scary, but the one teaching Norwegian and the other subjects is worse. She is a woman in her late forties with light colored hair and blue piercing eyes.

It is early in the day, and we have geography. We begin drawing on our maps the many rivers of the European continent. The teacher is wandering around assisting my classmates. I decide to raise my hand carefully, and I ask about one of the river outlets. The teacher looks at me with eyes that say, "You're annoyingly stupid." In a hurtful tone she announces, "Hello you guys, it is not like all the water in Europe flows downhill from the North Pole to Africa!" The whole classroom bursts into laughter. I am again so embarrassed. Why was I so stupid to raise my hand? I should have known better.

Suddenly, the anger wells up inside. If I thought that all the water in Europe flows downhill from north to south, why would I have been in doubt about the outlet? It would have been obvious!

I did not want to apply for high school. I would rather drop out of academic education than to stay in this situation!

In the end, my father nudges and encourages me to at least try out high school. He had been the one who helped me over-prepare for school for years, while at the same time endlessly trying to convince me that the teachers were there to help me learn.

Fast forward, I am 17 years old, and I am starting my second to last year in high school. With low self-esteem and next to no expectations for my school performance, I am okay with grades in the lower spectrum.

It's an ordinary Tuesday morning in early September. I am entering the school, and I see something across the staircase in the huge hallway. There is a big, dark blue stand with three young adults—a business school stand! I slowly approach one of the girls at the desk, a 22-year-old with short, dark hair.

"What is this?" I ask, surprised. She smiles at me, "Oh, we are from the Norwegian School of Management," she says enthusiastically. "This school is amazing! You do marketing, law, psychology, strategy, economy, mathematics, and it prepares you for whatever you want to specialize in later on. And afterwards you can work here in Norway, in Europe, in the US, or Australia!"

I am listening to this girl and my eyes are wide open. I feel like I have found the shiny pot at the end of the rainbow, or the golden ticket to Willy Wonka's Chocolate Factory—a ticket that lays the world at my feet.

Wow! Oh my gosh, I did not know something like this existed. I would absolutely love to do this. What must I do to go there? Then it dawns on me . . . I would need a higher level of mathematics, one of the subjects I didn't choose to do this year . . . plus, it would require a high grade average. This feels impossible. My heart contracts.

A few days pass, and I cannot get the vision of me going to that school out of my head. How amazing would it be to travel the world while working? I really do not want to lose this "ticket" to freedom. Is there anything I can do from where I am? Is there a way I can still attend the classes on mathematics, and strategically drop in? An even better thought comes to me. I guess I could manage to get a higher grade average if I *really* want it. And that's exactly what I do.

Within eight months, I finish my year with one of the highest grade averages in my class and I can tick off fulfilling the mathematics requirement, taken as an extra subject.

With a grateful heart, I realize the power of having a vision for what I wanted to get out of school. Now, every subject suddenly has a different meaning. Even English, which I feared the most, becomes playful, because now I envision myself speaking and writing in English after graduating from this business school, working around the world.

My mind had completely shifted from striving to thriving during those eight months. Not only did my grades improve, but my whole life. I met a wonderful boyfriend and made a friend for life; we still hang out. I took dance classes, started working in the local grocery store, and earned great money for a teen. I was creative, communicative, and alive. And I realized, the teachers didn't change, my school didn't change—I changed.

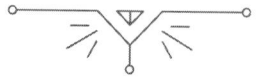

Reflections Don't Lie

Margie Zieigler
COLORADO, USA

I'm on the phone with my friend Susanna, telling her how closed in I feel. "There's new home construction going on next door. It is noisy. They're in my space." Susanna offers to make me some flower essences to help clear the feeling.

It's not the construction crowding me. All of this is a reflection of me and my life.

My love relationship can be emotionally painful. Although it has many beautiful qualities, it doesn't reflect the true essence of my soul.

It's stagnating and running its course, and closure is inevitable.

The years keep going by. I'm afraid of dying without ever having truly lived and shared this enormous love I hold in my heart.

It's January 1st. As I talk to my boyfriend in the kitchen, I know he has no intention of keeping his promises. I say, "It's another year. It's over. You've had fifteen years." Although we've had this conversation before, something is different today. I'm different.

I'm not crying. It feels sort of strange that I am past the tears today. This goodbye is unplanned. It simply has to be.

The door shuts. His vehicle starts and he drives away.

It's quiet.

I'm standing in my kitchen, gazing out the large picture window overlooking the half-frozen river and enchanting woods below. I see an image of me standing tall, far above the ground. In the vision, I am wearing jeans and a colorful silky iridescent cloak with mostly purples, reds, and blues. The woman I am in this image is at a higher level of being than ever before. I am confident and strong. It is the goddess-warrior part of me. At this point, I know that I will never revert to my old ways. Even though I love him dearly, I am not in harmony with the relationship.

Part of me, the goddess warrior, is the entrepreneurial woman pushing hard to create success. I deeply desire to take care of myself and empower myself financially. The opposing part of me is this little girl who longs to be nurtured, loved, and cared for.

I intend to start a whole new life.

It's time to follow through with something I've been saying for years. I am selling my home and moving to a place that gives me life every day. The part that pulls on my heartstrings is leaving Wisconsin, where my family, especially my daughters and granddaughter live.

I'm moving to Colorado. It's something that I dreamed up 25 years ago. I love the mountains. It's part of who I am and has been since I was a little girl.

I'm bringing a Golden Retriever pup into my life to be my companion. She's on my vision board.

Driving up to the farmhouse in Platteville, WI, I see acres for the dogs to run. The children bring the puppies in. I sit on the floor in the farmhouse and wait for the puppy who will choose me.

One puppy comes to me. I put my hands on her and she stays

with me. Decision made. I ask the Universe what to name her. I hear the name "Lulu." That was easy.

I'm selling my home, with forty-five days to clear it before closing.

My friend Shelley appears at my door. She's here to help me move things, donate, and discard. I cannot imagine doing this on my own.

Lulu and I travel westward. This entire journey is based on trust, trusting that the Universe has my back. Trusting my inner guidance.

We are settling into a motel in Boulder, Colorado, our base as we search for a place to live. Going from city to city, I realize it feels good right here. What I want is right under my nose. What perfect guidance to land right here.

Beholding a beautiful mountain view, I'm standing in the parking lot of my motel in Boulder. In my hand are the keys to my new condo and a new lease on life.

Lulu and I drive back to Wisconsin. I get to spend time with my beautiful daughters, celebrate my upcoming birthday, and gather my stuff.

I am so grateful to Shelley for offering to drive the moving truck to Colorado. She's staying for an entire week, helping me clean and settle in.

Now settled, I take her to the airport.

I'm on my own. For the first time, there is no one to fall back on. No parents. No husband. No man.

It's up to me. There is no one here to save me but me.

I declare, "In two years, I will stand strong on my own two feet."

It's now a time to let go of blame, guilt, resentment, and shame.

I lean into loving and accepting every aspect of my being, noticing thoughts and feelings, and continually calibrating. I am becoming happier within myself.

Having less space and less stuff is incredibly cleansing.

I love the open spaces and the beauty of the mountains. Lulu keeps me on my toes, getting me up early, and together we appreciate the spaciousness of the outdoors, with epic mountain views and trails right out my door. I learn so much from her and love her more every day.

I feel open and receptive.

I can breathe deeply.

I even released twenty excess pounds.

I love traveling back and forth to see my daughters and granddaughters.

Opportunities come for various entrepreneurial ventures. I listen to my intuition and choose what feels good to me.

I find myself using push energy again, listening to the plethora of marketing and business-building strategies of others for success. I take a step back to observe.

A new desire is born, a desire to pause. It's time to listen more intently to my inner voice. I tell the Universe that I am now open to receive.

I hear a voice saying, "This is your time. Breathe. You are taken care of. Enjoy your life, your granddaughters, your puppy, your time."

Pausing feels strange, yet I'm in harmony with it. I am allowing myself to receive the abundance that is here for me.

I'm in my dharma, enjoying what I do and give. My action is inspired.

I'm flowing with the rhythm of my own soul's guidance.

It's been two years, and I'm standing firmly on my own two feet. The goddess warrior part of me takes full responsibility for my life. The little girl in me loves, laughs, and nurtures my soul.

I love this adventure I am on.

The spaciousness I am experiencing reflects my life.

Something Even Better

Theresa Garvin Sudbury
MASSACHUSETTS, USA

As I collect the money for our final sale, I am feeling elated now that all of our furniture is sold, our yard sale was a huge success, and we are free to travel to Taiwan to teach English as a second language for the next year.

We are cleaning up my mother's driveway from the yard sale when my mother comes from her mailbox and hands me an envelope. The return address is YMCA of Greater Hartford. I am so excited and yell to Tim, "Our confirmation letter is here!" I think about our interview last month.

Tim and I sat with the YMCA director, and we shared about how we met working at the YMCA and got married this past September. I told him about my Master of Social Work degree, and how I have been working at a child guidance clinic since graduating. Tim proudly recounts his many accomplishments as the Director of Camp Mahackeno—the YMCA camp in Westport, Connecticut.

We both talk excitedly about our strong desire to travel, to be immersed in another culture, and to make a difference in the world.

For the past nine months, we have been researching and interviewing various volunteer organizations including Save the Children, and the United States Peace Corps. We admit that our dream is to serve in the Peace Corps, however, we're told that couples are rarely accepted, and that when they are, it is because they each have matching skills such as both being teachers or environmentalists.

While we feel disappointed about the Peace Corps, our dream, we decide to be open to the fabulous program through the YMCA—teaching English in Taiwan. We decide that this opportunity would also be life-changing, and we would love to do it.

As we conclude this interview, the director shakes each of our hands, and says, "I don't make the final decision, however, I make the recommendation, and the board typically accepts those I recommend. You two seem like a perfect fit for this. I will be highly recommending you." We smile ear to ear, and thank him repeatedly. As we walk down the hall, he yells, "Hey—send me a post card from Taiwan!" Tim and I get in the car and scream, "We're in!"

Coming back to the present moment, I tear open the envelope and my heart drops. I pass the rejection letter to Tim, who has an even bigger look of disbelief. We both stand there speechless as we look around our new temporary bedroom in my mother's home, and at the empty driveway . . . as our belongings have all just been sold. We have my Toyota Corolla left, and our clothes.

"Now what?" I ask.

Tim says, "Let's go get pizza." As we sit staring into space at the pizza shop, seemingly unaware that we are eating, we both keep repeating the same questions: "How could this happen?" "Why did this happen?" "What the heck?" and "Now what?" We feel lost beyond belief, confused, and embarrassed that we have gone this far without it working out. We cannot believe that we had this all planned out and executed everything before receiving written confirmation. We had only imagined our vision coming to fruition.

We are in a state of shock. No ideas, no solutions, and no other options or explanations come to mind for either of us. We finish our meal in sad silence and head back to my mom's house. I know that we need to share our news with her, but I am not sure how to answer when she asks, "What is the backup plan?"

We agree that something will work out. We are not willing or ready to accept that this is it, that our dream has just ended in a devastating disappointment. We decide to take a few days to decompress before making any other plans.

For the next two days, we are somber and quiet, and my mother is empathetic and supportive. My mother and Tim's mom are those people who love to say, "Things happen for a reason." At least they know not to say that right now.

On the third morning following our yard sale, the phone rings, and I answer. The voice on the line says, "Hello. Is this Theresa Garvin?"

I reply, "Yes," having no idea who it is.

"This is the New York City US Peace Corps office. Tim and you interviewed here a few months ago and well . . . we think we may have found a country that needs both of your skills, and they are happy to accept you two as a couple. It's Jamaica, the West Indies. They need a hospital social worker, and someone to work at the Boys and Girls Club. Are you and Tim still interested?" Tim was standing close enough to hear the conversation, and we both yell "Yes! Yes! We accept!"

We board our flight to Miami for a three-day staging process before heading to Kingston, Jamaica to begin our Peace Corps training and service. I am beaming and proudly telling anyone who will listen, "Today is our one-year wedding anniversary, and we are beginning our service in the US Peace Corps!"

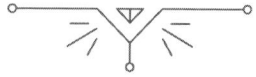

Be Still

Sharon Tala
NEW HAMPSHIRE, USA

One morning with the sunshine beaming through the window, three-year-old Nathan, Hannah, his baby sister, and I are eating breakfast—warm, hearty oatmeal with fresh berries. I begin reciting this simple, powerful phrase aloud, encouraging Nathan to repeat after me, "Be still . . ."

"Be still," he repeats.

Next, I add, "Be still . . . and know that I am God."

Then Nathan repeats after me in his sweet little voice, "Be still and know that I am God." With excitement and a big smile, he recites it after me again.

We say these words together a few more times. As I clap to celebrate his accomplishment, both Nathan and Hannah clap, along with giggles and hugs!

Fast forward a few months, and I find myself in the "we-can't-be-late-for-school" frantic rush. Since Nathan was born, he was a calm, easygoing, loving soul. It was the first thing people noticed about him. This morning sweet Nathan is taking his time dressing himself in his l'il man preppy blue-and-yellow plaid shirt and khaki shorts. Before we step out the door, I tie Nathan's sneakers so we can be on our merry way. Only it wasn't that merry of a morning, as I feel frazzled. While Nathan sits on the front step with his carefree, wiggly legs kicking and swinging to what seems to be a silent musical tune, I yank his shoestrings and bark at him, "Be still!"

Without skipping a beat or batting an eyelash, Nathan replies in his precious voice, ". . . and know that I am God."

Talk about being stopped in my tracks—I realize I'm the one who needs to be still. The hamster running the hectic morning show in my head got off its wheel and took a long-overdue deep breath. Time-out! I breathe into the present moment and reset myself. Stunned as I am, surprisingly, my heart feels comforted and supported. At that moment, I realize that when I get caught up in the hamster wheel, there is great wisdom in the art of being still that connects me to My Creator, allowing inner peace to expand within me. This vital truth will be a guiding factor down the road.

For most of my adult life, I've faithfully supported my husband's vocational ministry in various ways. I thought we were answering our spiritual calling. However, I began to realize that for him, it was more important to appear spiritual than to be spiritual. I knew there was something strange about the marriage, but I could not put my finger on it.

I had been counseling women in toxic relationships. When researching, I saw a video of a pastor's wife speaking about covert toxicity disguised as spirituality that rang true to me. There was no denying that woman echoed my inner voice, which wasn't so quiet any longer. Once again, the hamster got a jolt as the wheel screeched to a halt. Tuning into the stillness, I was devastated to discover that my husband and I were not on the same path in life, and I realized all my efforts to save the marriage were futile.

This realization led me to understand more about my values. Traditional values to me meant that couples stayed married for better or for worse. To this day, I still embrace my traditional values, yet I learned they are way more meaningful when the person you're with embodies those same values. That gracious "Be still" voice gave me the insight, strength, and peace to find my safety outside that marriage. It is not only okay but necessary to prioritize your safety, and this was not at odds with my values.

In legal discussions, it becomes evident that there will be no support for me or our college-age kids. How will I provide for my children and myself after being a stay-at-home mom for over two decades? I calmly remind myself to "be still" and trust that everything will work out for the best. Even in these darkest moments, my stillness brings me peace, knowing that, at last, I am safe physically, spiritually, emotionally, and mentally.

Seeking to start my life anew, I take a class to strengthen me on my spiritual journey where we practice a meditation for 40 days. On the second day, clarity shines forth! It is one of the most positive, life-affirming moments I have ever experienced.

I hear a clear voice from within me: "After all those years and everything you put into that marriage, you have nothing. No home. No savings. No job. No assets. No one to save you. You have nothing. Girl, you are what most consider rock bottom. But what you do have are you and God. And you know what? That is all you need. There is no better place for you to be. You no longer have anything to define who you are or to give you some sense of security—a false sense of security."

Dire as the message sounds, it was soothing and inspiring to me. I realized I am more than a job, a house, a bank account, etc.—all the things that society uses to define a person. No longer having any of those things created a space for me to see who I really am. I wasn't losing anything. I was actually gaining . . . gaining perspective and freedom—freedom to be who I am.

I am a clean slate. I am thankful for the opportunity to grow beyond the restrictions of past programming and expectations of who I should be. Now that I have learned to love and honor myself, I am more able to love others wholeheartedly.

In that meditative stillness, soul-cleansing tears of freedom and indescribable peace flow from me. I am empowered, knowing I have absolutely *everything* I need within me. The stillness that gave me very close relationships with my kids has healed the most forgotten relationship of my life—the one with myself. I can now be in a full expression of my heart, mind, and spirit.

When it all falls away, we can see ourselves with fresh eyes. We are more worthy and gifted than we believe. We are far more capable than we fathom. We are so much more than we can imagine!

I am focused on the rest of my life being the best of my life. From time to time, the hamster starts spinning that wheel. When it does, I remember to speak to it in a loving voice: "Be still and know that I am God."

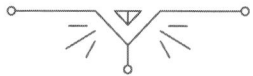

Bread Baking Challenge

Mary K. Ott
NEW JERSEY, USA

"Follow your dreams and the path will follow," the deep, reverberating voice says, and the screen cuts to black.

I close out the tab on YouTube and sigh.

That's what I've been told to do my whole life, but it's always confused me.

It's not that I don't love to do things.

In fact, it's the opposite—I love to do everything, to be everywhere, and to experience the richness of life.

In the movies, a clear-cut path always appears magically for the dreamer. I need something fulfilling to do—but what? I ponder, "Maybe I could go back to school and get a degree in therapy, psychology, or neuroscience." Then I realize I would be in a classroom, opening a notebook next to someone the same age as my own children.

I could spend my days on a laptop, writing life into stories that I love. Or maybe I could travel place-to-place, inspiring crowds at public speaking events.

But then, maybe I should teach art at the local elementary

school. Those art projects with my kids have always been my favorite memories.

Maybe I could just do all of them? Why do they make it seem like it's so easy to pick a profession at the age of five and stick with it?

As I went down to the kitchen to make tea, a new idea for a possible profession began brewing with each creak of the stairs. As I was pouring hot water from the kettle into my teacup, a spark of inspiration hit. I could make my own 30-day challenge. I love playing fun games and it would bring much-needed joy to the situation.

What should it be? I looked around the room for ideas. I needed something unfamiliar enough that it felt like a challenge, but also something familiar enough for me to feel confident right away. My eye caught on the jar of flour sitting on the counter. Well, of course. Cooking and baking was already therapeutic for me.

Competition: myself.

Challenge: bake bread.

Duration: 30 days.

I will call it my "success in one area leads to success in other areas 30-day challenge."

The doorknob rattles, and my daughter emerges from her cave, where she hides for 14 hours a day, so I tell her the idea.

"That sounds nice." She just tilts her head and shrugs. She's my biggest cheerleader.

I get out my old recipe books, look at what's new online, and gather up all my ingredients. I start at the basics with the easy breads. I get creative with what I add: sunflower seeds, cranberries, and walnuts.

Then I move on to more complicated breads. Some of these have to sit overnight in the fridge or use techniques I'm not used to. I make the breads of my childhood—Ukrainian Easter Babka and Poppy Seed Roll. I try breads from different places around the world.

Do you know that bread was a means to community in basically every culture? Bread wasn't just something to eat—it was a way to unite families, to signify meaning, and a staple during easy and hard times.

Near the end of the second week, I make a braided vegan challah bread. I make two loaves and bring one to share with a friend.

"You made this? Wow, it's outstanding. Don't tell her I said this, but it might even be more delicious than my mother's home-made challah bread. What's your secret?"

I ponder momentarily. I am a great baker because I make it with love, and the fact that I love baking bread. I decide to share my story about my "success leads to more success" challenge.

In these 30 days, I create so much fun and enjoyment from baking and sharing my breads. I am so pleased with my success that I have empowering moments of inspiration. I wonder what else I can accomplish by playing a bigger game and getting increasingly better each time.

Before I know it, it is all over much sooner than I expect. Yet, I don't stop there. Why not start another challenge? I run out and buy new paints, brushes, and canvas. As soon as my front door closes, I immediatcly start painting. I feel liberated from the adrenaline of unbridled artistic expression. Joy and gratitude fill me up.

An idea for a bigger game crosses my mind. It touches my heart and soul with tingles. I know what I want to do! I know what I am good at!

I realize what I have been doing all along. Through empowering myself, I was able to empower others. I love to help people, to listen, to share their stories and experiences. I feel at home when I am encouraging others to be their best self. I love to be their cheerleader.

And if I could do that for a living, it would bring me all the joy in the world. I immediately begin to investigate for days. I want to travel, meet people from different backgrounds, heal hearts, and build friendships.

I sign up for an international transformational life coaching certification program. I know I am going to love this. This is a goal worthy of my dreams. It is going to be as inspiring, fun, and fulfilling as I imagine. I will get to do what I love every day.

And for the next 30 days, and the 30 days after that, and the 30 days after that. I will continue to explore and expand in the field of coaching. Instead of bread, I get to see my clients rise in power. Instead of using colorful paint, I get to see the vibrancy explode in other peoples' lives. And, I still get to bake bread between clients.

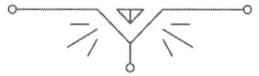

Sixty Seconds

Amanda Beswick
UNITED KINGDOM

I sit bolt upright, my heart beating wildly, my mouth dry. I must have nodded off—albeit briefly. I glance over at the bedside clock. It's 1:00 in the morning. I am wide awake. A feeling of panic rises up from the pit of my stomach as the all-too-familiar voice in my head starts its nightly rant: "So, how are you going to pay the rent now that you're the only one earning? Not to mention the food shopping . . . the fuel for the car . . . the heating bills . . ." The voice is getting increasingly frantic and hysterical.

I feel sick and rush to the bathroom. Sitting on the side of the bath, I think back to how only six months after moving to a new area, finding the perfect home, and filled with excitement at the prospect of starting a new life together, it had all been taken away with one brief but crushing phone call. My partner, who until recently had been the main breadwinner, had not only lost his job but was now sinking ever deeper into a state of apathy and self-pity with no inclination to look for a new opportunity or seek help for his condition.

I sink to the floor, my head in my hands, and reflect on how every night I act out the same exhausting scene, a bad dream from which I am unable to wake up and escape. The tumbling into bed feeling hopeless and beaten and falling instantly asleep. The being jolted awake, what seems like only minutes later, by the voice of my fear, and knowing, with sickening certainty, that there will be no more sleep for me tonight.

I creep downstairs, not wanting to disturb my sleeping partner, and make a drink to distract myself. A few weeks ago, I would have opened a bottle of wine in the hope of putting myself into a stupor and passing out. I've stopped that now. It didn't have the desired effect, plus I can't afford it.

Thoughts of how much I dislike my job overwhelm me. The lonely twice-daily 90-minute commute that ends in a grey and soulless car park. The bank of desks and monitors where I take my seat day after day in a windowless corner of a vast open office filled with people with whom I feel no connection.

I think back to when I took the job, telling myself that it would be temporary, just something to tide us over whilst we got settled in. Now, I feel trapped. This is the only income we have, and it barely covers the bills, even though we are now living in a cheaper place. We moved out of our lovely new home—we couldn't afford to stay there.

I feel tears flowing down my face as I travel down the well-worn path of self-pity and blame. "Why does life have to be such a struggle? It's not fair. How come other people seem to have it all and here I am with a job I hate, a cold, damp house and a partner who doesn't care about anything anymore. Is this really the best that life can offer me?"

I shake myself. "This won't do, Amanda! Remember your breath is your friend, now breathe . . ."

Some hours later, I am parking my car and heading through the revolving doors that lead to the office. I feel empty and numb as I wind my way through the sea of desks and faceless people towards my seat. As I get closer, however, my attention is caught by the buzz of excitement coming from my team, who are all gathered around a desk at the far end of the room. Voices are raised, but I can't quite make out any words. I am curious.

I approach the group. Nobody looks at me, nobody says good morning. I catch the words, "That's a huge pay raise!" Then another voice pipes up, "Yes, and they get to choose what hours they work." "Unbelievable!" exclaims another colleague. "I mean, they already earn more than the job warrants. They're on a cushy number!"

My curiosity turns to a feeling of urgency. I have to find out what is causing such a stir amongst my team members. Somehow, I just know deep inside—*this matters.*

My heart is in my mouth, but I am feeling determined as I approach a colleague. My voice cracks as I ask him, "Hey Richard, what's all the fuss about this morning?" He turns to me in surprise and says, "Don't you read the news?" He waves a newspaper at me and points to a headline so I can see which industry sector he is referring to as he says, "These guys are getting a huge pay raise for basically doing very little. I'm in the wrong job!" And with that he pushes the newspaper into my hands and marches over to his desk, shaking his head in disbelief.

As I stare down at the large black typeface, something extraordinary happens. Time stands still. The background noise of the office becomes hushed. I'm no longer aware of where I am. There is just me and the headline. I know it is trying to tell me something. Shouting it, in fact!

And then I feel it. The Shift. I can almost hear the click of a switch as a light goes on in my mind and I see everything so clearly.

As my thoughts crystallize, I know with absolute certainty that if other people can have a job they love, where they earn a great salary and can choose their own hours, then so can I. It takes me just 60 seconds to make a decision. A life-affirming, powerful move that says, "I am back in the game, stronger than ever before. That job has my name on it and nothing is going to prevent me from going out and claiming it."

The moment passes; the noise and sights and sounds of the office come rushing back in as I sit down at my desk. It all looks the same on the surface, but I am aware that something momentous has just taken place. I am not the same person who walked in through that office door. I am the new, empowered, expansive me. There is a light in my eyes and a fire in my heart. I have a purpose and a goal and a one-way ticket to a bright new future.

A Breath-Taking Dream
into Another World

Sonia Ovenden
QATAR

The floor-to-ceiling photographs are incredible, as if taken straight from National Geographic. They are mesmerizing, and the iridescent colors are magical. Some images are simple to identify—sharks, lionfish, and turtles, though some I've never seen before. For as long as I can remember, I've dreamed of diving in warm waters exploring the vast array of sea life. I can almost hear the bubbles the regulator would make as I breathe underwater, not needing to surface for air. Turning my attention to the lady standing behind the slightly worn counter, I hold my breath.

"Sorry, we can't get you insurance with asthma. So, we're unable to train you to become a certified scuba diver," she explains with a small frown.

My heart plummets as I hear the same message I've already received from two other dive centers. Before I leave, I scan the underwater pictures covering the wall one last time. My desire to scuba dive has never wavered until right now.

At thirteen, I was diagnosed with asthma. People believed I wouldn't be good at sports. And often, out of fear, I was discouraged to even try. Yet instead of being limited by my abilities, I chose to have the condition rather than the condition having me.

Asthma never stops me from doing anything—a twenty-four-hour swimathon for charity, playing netball, dancing, working out, or even completing a ten-kilometer road race. But this time feels different; perhaps it's finally beaten me; should I let it go? After all, I'm being told no, it's not possible.

It reminds me of one of my favorite quotes by Audrey Hepburn: "Nothing is impossible; the word itself says 'I'm possible!'"

At that moment, I enter the land of possibilities. There must be a way. My desire and my passion for exploring the oceans are too strong to ignore. I dream of visiting the underwater world, and surely the dream would have dwindled away if it wasn't meant for me. I mean, "Finding Nemo" would make anyone want to scuba dive, right?

I expand the current "no" and change it to "not yet."

As I sit by the pool in Kuwait, the sun is warming my skin, and my eyes squint behind my oversized sunglasses. I see the ocean, knowing I belong there, knowing one day I'll dive into the deep blue sea and be at one with the underwater world. I won't accept no for an answer.

With my phone in hand, I press the internet icon, and type in "scuba diving insurance providers." The word DAN is prominent in the search results, and I learn it's one of the major providers. I press the email button and ask what I could do to become a certified scuba diver despite my asthma. I include all the things it has never kept me from doing.

I'm afraid if I hear another "no" the chance to realize my dream will pass me by. I dread that the answer I might receive could mean the end. Yet, my overwhelming desire pulls me along. So,

I cross my fingers, press send and set the intention for a favorable response.

"What you up to?" says Kevin as he pokes me in the ribs.

"Nothing much. Fancy a swim?"

"Definitely," he says, wiping the sweat from his neck.

We swim, laugh, and splash for a few minutes, though I can't relax. I'm holding my breath, both literally and figuratively. A few minutes later, we climb out of the pool and plonk our wet bodies on the ocean blue-colored towels . . . I mean, really, as if I needed a reminder that my dream was in the balance.

Kevin reaches for the menu and calls over the server.

"I'll have a vanilla milkshake, please," I say.

The server nods and places the order as I reach into my beach bag for my phone. I close my eyes and whisper a prayer, "Please let there be a way."

I click on my emails, and the response is at the top. I pause and take a slow breath, stroking my fingertips against my palm. "What if my dream dies?" My thoughts are racing. "What if it's a no again?" My internal chatter subsides as an empowering thought finally lands. "What if it's not?" and immediately I open the email.

I scan it once, twice, and then a third time.

"Wow, wow, wow," I say, as I drop my phone on the sunbed and jump into the pool.

Kevin watches and swiftly jumps into the pool too. He swims up to me and smiles.

"What's happened, babe?"

"I can train to become a certified scuba diver," I say, laughing and crying.

"Sonia, you know we've tried, but you can't get insurance."

"No, you don't understand. I contacted a company earlier today, and they've just emailed back, saying all I need to do is get a doctor to confirm I'm fit to dive, and they will insure me," I explain quickly.

"Do you believe you can do that?"

"Absolutely! In the email, they even said as much when I explained my current level of fitness."

He hugs me, almost squeezing the air out of my lungs. You see, while it was a dream of mine, it ignited a desire in him to become a certified scuba diver, too—we shared the dream all along.

And now we share the reality. Fifteen years later, we walk along the beach back to the dive center, my flippers and mask in one hand and my empty nitrox tank bouncing gently on my back. The Maldivian sun starts its descent, casting a tangerine glow across the sky.

"That was amazing," Kevin says.

"Which part? The part where I learned how close you must get to a six-foot shark to annoy it? Or the Bat Fish following our bubbles, or the ghost pipe fish hovering in the fern?" I chuckle.

"Well, all of that, but mostly that we've just done our three hundredth dive," he says, taking my hand.

"And to think, I almost gave up this dream," I say through tears.

"I'm so glad you didn't, babe." He squeezes my hand.

"Me too."

So, when you have a burning desire and you face a no, ask yourself, what can you do from where you are with what you have? There will *always* be a way.

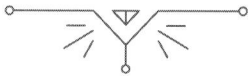

The Courage to Choose

Stephanie Puente
COLORADO, USA

The cursor blinks in the empty Google search bar. My gaze is fixed on the computer screen and my hands rest on the keyboard. I have a desire to find a marathon to run in and it keeps tugging at my heart. Although being a mom of two incredible daughters brings me tremendous joy, a part of me feels like I'm not growing and my soul is yearning to do something just for me. I would love to run in a race in a beautiful location that my family can enjoy too. I'm about to start my search and think, "Wait, this will be an expensive trip and all of our resources are already committed to cover our monthly expenses. This is a luxury we can't afford."

Curiosity wins over practicality and I type "Top 10 marathons in the US" into the search bar. A list appears, and a race catches my attention: Big Sur International Marathon. I click on it and a promotional video begins to play a visual feast before my eyes. The race is along the Pacific Coast Highway. It's lined with gorgeous redwoods. Waves crash along the beach. It crosses a spectacular bridge with a view to an amazing rock out in the ocean. Along the route, there's a man in a tuxedo playing beautiful music on a grand piano. I am sold and exclaim out loud, "I would love to run in this race!" Another part of me thinks, "How do we do this without going into debt? How long will it take to save for this trip? I have no time to train! Is this an unrealistic idea? Am I being selfish?"

I push aside these thoughts, take a deep breath, and walk into the living room to share this with my husband. "I want to run in the Big Sur International Marathon, and I want our family to come too." At first, he's hesitant, uncertain about how we can do it. After a quiet pause, he says, "Okay."

We have enough cash to cover the race registration fee. I submit my payment and rejoice at the message that pops onto the screen, "Congratulations, you're registered!" With enthusiasm I get busy selecting a training plan and start running.

Every Sunday night, I feel proud as I cross off how far I've run that week. With excitement, I review what's next on my workout schedule to build my strength and mileage. I'm surprised to discover that there is time for me to train and the exercise is helping me to be a more grounded and present mom.

A voice continues to shout in my head, "Where will the rest of the money come from?" I choose to focus on celebrating the miles I've run, and an idea comes to open a California Vacation Checking Account. This action feels like a signal to the Universe that we are creating space for the resources to flow in. I walk into the bank and even though my inner critic is saying, "This is so stupid!" I open the account.

As my training progresses, my husband and I explore cities along the coast that we'd love to visit. We schedule fun activities in our calendar to do while we're there with the girls, and we invite my mother-in-law and my dad to join us. Doubt gets louder in my mind and I wonder, "What if we can't go?" Instead of entertaining the doubt, I choose to visualize us being there. While running on my neighborhood streets, I imagine crossing the finish line, finishing strong and waving to my family, who are cheering me on.

When I am with my friends, I share, "We're going to California and I'm running in a marathon!" Out of the blue, one friend says, "I sold some gold coins that were laying around my house and I got quite a bit of money for them." This sparks an idea. I have some jewelry that I co-own with my sister that neither of us wants, and it's been sitting in my closet for eight years.

I take the jewelry to three different stores and settle on a wonderful offer. My heart fills with joy as I leave the shop with a few thousand dollars in hand. After splitting the money with my sister, there is more than enough left over to pay for the rest of our trip.

The marathon weekend arrives and it seems surreal. It feels like I'm floating up the steps of the expo hall as I pick up my race bib and goody bag. I'm overcome as I think, "I'm living my dream!"

The morning of the race, tears fill my eyes as I stand at the starting line. The gun goes off and I run past the redwoods. I hear the waves crashing against the beach. I see the man in the tuxedo at the grand piano and hear his beautiful music. The spectacular bridge that sparked this dream comes into view. I keep running and at the last mile, I feel a renewed sense of strength as the finish line appears. The announcer calls out on the loud speaker, "Coming on strong is Stephanie Puente. Stephanie Puente, Number 2907 from Lakeway, Texas!" With pride I wave to my family who are there on the sidelines cheering me on. I cross the finish line and embrace my husband and daughters as we savor this moment.

Our trip comes to a close, and as we board the plane for the flight home, I reflect on how this experience has impacted my life. The value of our moments together in the redwoods, on a boat ride under the Golden Gate Bridge, and walking along the Pacific coastline are priceless. Despite the potential negative conditions I perceived, I chose to follow my heart even when I couldn't see the path forward. I have discovered that when I take the step that I can take, that's how the next step appears. I am so grateful to know that the doorway to new possibilities is always open, but I have to be willing to recognize it and choose to walk through the door.

End of Watch

Laura Corkery
TEXAS, USA

My phone rings, startling me. It's late. My baby and toddler are sleeping. I see it's a coworker, so I answer. Before I can speak, I hear, "Is your husband okay?" I look at my husband lying next to me and say, "Yes, why? What's happening?"

She says, "Turn on the news."

Scott, hearing every word, turns on the news. My stomach drops. There is an active shooter in downtown Dallas, minutes from our house. I feel sick. Multiple police officers have been shot, maybe fatally. I am glued to the screen as my husband, a Dallas Police Officer, turns on his radio. It's chaos.

Scott turns to me and says, "I have to go in." I tell him, "Please, just wait. Everyone's going in if they aren't there already. It's late. You worked all day, and you'll be back in a few hours. Someone's going to have to relieve everyone there now." We are afraid for those we love on shift tonight and stay up trying to understand what is happening. At 2:00 AM, exhausted, we give up and go to bed.

It feels like only moments later, and I'm up. I drop our babies at daycare and head to work. I'm numb. I'm in shock. Five officers are dead, and nothing makes sense. Scott left before I woke up. He's an Honor Guard member, and they will stay with the fallen 24/7 until they've been laid to rest.

I park and turn off the car. My heart sinks as I think about walking into the building. I have no idea why I'm at work. I head to my office and sit down. My former manager comes around the corner and wraps me in a hug. She asks if I'm okay. Her husband used to work in Law Enforcement, and she gets it. She gets how terrifying it is, how personal it feels. She says, "I'm surprised you even came in."

I'm at work for a few hours, and I decide I can't do this. I feel wrung out and empty. I don't know where I need to be right now, but I know it isn't here. I walk out and head home on autopilot.

Friends and family call and ask me if we are okay. Are we okay? I don't even know anymore. I knew when Scott became a police officer there would be risk. He straps on a gun to go to work. I know he could be injured or killed on the job. He could be shot responding to a domestic violence call or killed while working a traffic accident. I never thought he might be killed simply because of the uniform. His desire to serve people in their darkest moments could cause me to lose him forever. It suddenly becomes real. July 7th has changed everything.

Scott has been on the job for seven years, but we don't have many "police friends." I realize how isolated I feel. Who can I call that is going to understand what I am feeling right now? I check in with my husband. He doesn't know when he can be home, but it will be late. Dallas PD has never experienced a loss like this. There aren't enough Honor Guard members to cover everything without working long days. Everyone is called in, and they are stretched thin.

The next few days pass in a haze. Scott is gone before I get up, and I go to bed alone each night. There are viewings and vigils. They are planning the funerals. The only way I can see Scott is to attend these events, but I don't want to be a distraction. He is performing Honor Guard duties and won't have time to see me except for a few stolen minutes before or after services. Should I attend the funerals? I didn't know the officers. Is it still okay to go? Will the families not want strangers there? The thoughts race through my head. The phone rings. My friend, Liz, is calling. "Hey, how are you?" she asks, concern lacing her voice.

"I don't know. I'm trying to decide if I am going to the funerals. I'm so confused, and I don't know anyone who will be there."

"I'll go with you," she offers.

"Are you sure?" I ask.

"Absolutely," she responds.

I take a deep breath and walk into the church. I find a spot, and Liz meets me. I watch as people stream in and find seats. We are in the largest church I have ever seen. It's a sea of blue and black. I've never seen this many officers in one place, including Scott's graduation from the academy.

Pictures of the fallen officer flash on the large screen. The balcony is full of law enforcement officers from all over the country. They come to honor him. We listen to stories from his partner about how he met his wife and earned his nickname. There are tears and laughter. He was a person with a full life taken too soon. Not just a badge number. Not just a uniform.

Before this, I didn't understand why Scott wanted to be a member of the Honor Guard. He tried out three times to earn his spot.

Now, as I watch him stand by the casket, present colors, and serve his blue family, I get it. I want to know who these officers were. I want to honor them and their families. I don't want them to be just a name or a picture on a memorial somewhere. They deserve more.

I attend as many funerals as possible: Senior Corporal Lorne Ahrens, Sergeant Michael Smith, Officer Michael Krol, and Officer Patrick Zamarripa. I miss Officer Brent Thompson's service since it's on the same day as another funeral. After Sergeant Smith's service, I go to the gravesite. I stand in whatever shade I can find as the hot sun beats down. The last radio call plays. I hear the dispatcher notify all elements, "Badge number 6141 is out of service. End of Watch July 7, 2016. Godspeed, Mike." The tears roll down my face.

I meet other police spouses as I volunteer at vigils and attend viewings and funerals. We hold each other up. We mourn together. It feels like the start of a new chapter. I realize, even in the darkest hour, there is light. I am not alone in this. I begin to understand. My officer was not killed that night, but five brave officers and countless more ran toward gunfire to protect people. They are my family, too.

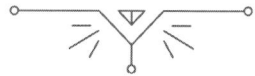

Two Pink Lines

Kassy Scarcia
MARYLAND, USA

Is that a second line? That can't be a second line. This test has to be defective. It's so faint, I'm sure it's a false positive. What am I going to do?

Holding the positive pregnancy test in my hand, the cold bathroom floor under my feet, my unsuspecting boyfriend sitting outside the door innocently playing video games, I stare at my reflection in the mirror, frozen with panic.

I thought for sure the test would be negative. That's why I didn't even tell my boyfriend I was taking one. I have felt off the last few weeks and I gained some weight—I've been blaming that on the Christmas cookies—but the chance of this test being positive never entered my mind. I simply wanted to put my girl brain at ease.

My mind is anything but at ease right now.

I know I have to open the bathroom door and ask my boyfriend if he sees a second line too, but once I do that our lives may never be the same. What if he freaks out? What if he immediately panics and bolts?

I wouldn't blame him. We talk about kids, but not now. Not yet. We have so many adventures left to experience together, dreams to pursue, mistakes to make, laughs to enjoy.

What are we going to do?

I take the biggest deep breath of my life, turn the cold door handle, and see him sitting in his oversized computer chair, not a care in the world. As I walk toward him, the only thing that I can think to say is, "Don't freak out, but do you see a second line?"

He looks at me, he looks down at the pregnancy test I just laid on his desk, and then back up at me. "Um, I mean maybe, but barely. Care to explain why I am looking at a pregnancy test?"

I fill him in on my girl brain, the last 20 minutes of my panic and being completely terrified to open that bathroom door. We both agree, wanting to live in denial, that this has to be a false positive and we just need another test to prove it.

Only problem? It's almost 11 PM and most stores are closed. Here goes the hardest seven-hour wait of my life.

The next morning, 5:55 AM, alarm bells go off on my cell phone. My boyfriend jumps out of bed, throws on a sweatshirt, and heads to the first drugstore down the street that opens at 6 AM.

All I can do is lay here, blankets curled up around me, my mind doing mental somersaults thinking of babies, college tuition, stretch marks . . .

He's finally back. I grab the box of tests out of his hand and escape into the bathroom before he can even say a word.

Thirty seconds. That's all it took. I saw the two—certainly not faint this time—pink lines and knew living in my denial world was no longer an option.

I'm pregnant. Like actually pregnant. What am I going to do? What is he going to do?

I painstakingly open the cold bathroom door handle once again, this time to him sitting on the bed staring at me, waiting to confirm whether our lives are about to change forever.

I look at him—he is calm, collected, steady—and I instantly crumble. Leaning against the hallway wall, I fall to the floor in fear, with tears running down my face. I have prayed to be a mom for so long, but not like this. Not before I am ready. Not with someone I have only been with for a year. Not before my business has flourished and I accomplish the things I am supposed to.

A few hours go by. I call my doctor and he agrees to take pity on me and get me in immediately to see how far along I am.

As I am sitting in the waiting area, a woman about eight months pregnant sits down two chairs away. With tears still bubbling up in my eyes thinking of all of the what-if's, I can't help but keep glancing in her direction. Thinking about my future, what pregnancy will be like, what I will feel like eight months from now.

The nurse opens the door to the hallway, calls my name, and takes me back to the ultrasound room. I lay on the cold exam table, lift up my shirt to give her access to my belly and stare up at the ceiling. Before I know it she is putting cold goo on my stomach, pressing down, clicking some buttons, and all of a sudden . . .

. . . thump thump, thump thump, thump thump.

There's a heartbeat.

A heartbeat of a little person inside of me. A gift I have prayed for for so many years, so unsure if it would happen because of my endometriosis, and yet here I am listening to a heartbeat come from my stomach. I am in shock, in awe, in disbelief.

As I drive back home from the doctor, alone in my car with just the country songs on the radio, I have all kinds of thoughts running through my head. Fears of the unknown. Worry about the pressure on our relationship. Anxiety over what our family will think. Nervousness about any complications. Doubts about my ability to be a mom right now. Sadness for the life I will miss out on and how many changes there will be.

But in the midst of all of that noise—all of that mindset chaos—I realize the most important piece.

This little human inside of me is my version of a miracle, and sometimes the universe takes us down a different path to our desired destination than we planned. But that different path can be even more beautiful than we could have imagined.

This little person isn't going to be the thing that hinders my life or derails it, she's going to be the thing that gives me more meaning and purpose than ever. She is going to be the thing that motivates me to never give up on my dreams or my passions because she deserves a mom living vibrantly in this world so that she can too one day.

The Unstoppable Power of Desire

Besim Can Onel

CANADA

My so-far short experience in Tokyo is already very unique.

The city is different from what I had imagined. The people are very kind and shy.

My first shopping experience turns into a big failure, which I can laugh at now. I could not use any of the things I bought, and I finish the night with a snack.

I live in a dormitory with students from different countries and in a non-English speakers environment. This includes my landlord. I am on my own, adding up unique experiences.

I am lost in the same subway train station twice a day for one week.

My motivation to learn Japanese is through the roof, so I can improve my life quality and enjoy the people and culture. I work hard every day to get better.

Today marks my being in Japan for six months. My Japanese developed at a rapid pace. I am now in the lower intermediate class. Next month, I am moving to the intermediate level. I am taking a

Japanese proficiency test, second level, with the encouragement of my Japanese language teacher.

My part-time job at embassy reception pays me back, greatly helping to improve my Japanese. I answer many incoming calls and share information, or direct people to a specific department. I am also working at two other part-time jobs to support my stay.

I have a busy weekday schedule, and I enjoy my weekends. I pass the second-level Japanese proficiency test. I speak and understand the language better, and socialize with Japanese friends.

When I look back on the last nine months, I can see the busy life I have built here. Being away and on my own feels good, and I realize I am out of my usual patterns. I do not harm myself here.

As an abused child when I was in grade two or three, I was unclear about what happened. I had never told anyone. I had nobody around to tell. I was staying with my grandparents. My mother had a health issue, and my father worked long hours.

I am considering extending my stay in Japan, taking a couple of more years to establish a better pattern of behavior, away from my regular environment. I have the desire to stay in Japan. I feel connected with the culture, being distant in a specific type of honesty. Being out of the vicious circle feels good and my burden is lighter.

I am looking for jobs and new experiences with discoveries about this new land and society. There are limited job options for a foreigner in Japan. I have tried using connections and have applied for different types of jobs. I am confident I can find a job with my credentials and my Japanese proficiency level and make enough to live. My feasibility study and the offers I have from my job search do not match. The job offers are under the minimum number. It is frustrating to hear the same conversation again and again. I am left out with the returning home option as the original plan.

I have three months left before I am supposed to return. My Japanese proficiency level is improving. I am now in the upper intermediate; after two months, I will be moving to the advanced level.

When you have a limited amount of time left, everything tends to move faster. As the time to leave draws closer, I am feeling heavier. There has to be a way to stay longer! I have less than a month left.

It's hard to accept one year has passed since I came to Japan, and I am going back next week. I had my farewell with my teachers and administrative staff.

The next step is the embassy. I have been procrastinating about the visit, fighting with the inner voice constantly telling me that I need to go and see, meet and greet the people at the embassy in person. I do not feel like going. A big battle is going on inside of me.

There is no time left. I am scheduled to return the next day. My embassy visit has to be today.

I walk into the embassy and greet people as I meet them, sharing that I am returning home, extending my gratitude. I feel devastated inside.

Meanwhile, I hear the assistant ambassador calling my name. I start to walk towards the stairs and see him calling for me. It is not common for him to talk to me. As I get closer, he starts talking, saying a person from a giant Japanese automotive manufacturing company wants to talk to me.

I am still determining why the assistant ambassador is teasing me. I find it painful. He is insisting I should take the phone. I resist, knowing he is playing with me. He is telling me this person on the other end of the phone is seeking a qualified resource, a mechanical engineer who can speak Japanese. The assistant ambassador is about to deny my availability, hears my voice, and realizes I am a perfect match.

I take the phone and start talking to the caller in Japanese. The company is investing in a manufacturing plant and looking for a Japanese-speaking mechanical engineer to hire and train in Japan for two years.

I am invited for an interview the next day, my return day. I know the company location, but I can't catch my plane if I go to the interview. I tell him my situation, but he insists that I have an interview when I am back home. So, I give him my contact information.

I am unsure what to expect. I am both confused and hopeful. I am busy fitting a year-long life into two suitcases and forget what happened earlier.

I arrive home after an over-twenty-hour flight, transfer, and wait time, and my father comes to pick me up at the airport. We chat for a while, and he mentions that someone has been calling me while I was traveling, and that he left his contact information. This is the call for the interview. I am shocked but grateful for how things are moving in my direction.

I sign a contract with the company, and in two days I am heading back to Japan.

Japan, wait for me. Our time is not over yet . . .

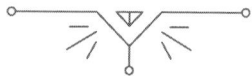

Operation Revelation!

Yvette Wright Gauff
NEW YORK, USA

Standing in the mirror pondering my image, my eyes lock on my abdomen. I trace the long scar there, the result of surgery to save my life. A simple line with a period underneath. My exclamation mark, a positive spin on a negative ordeal.

"The mark used in writing to indicate intensity of emotion, or loudness, after a statement that is an abrupt, forceful utterance or an outcry, as of protest." As the memorial of years of my body crying out in protest, calling my scar an exclamation point seems appropriate.

For some unknown reason, my body stopped working properly. In the morning, I look in the mirror, and by the day's end what I see is different: there is less hair on my head, less weight on my body, and my skin color has changed to the color of concrete.

I do not have time for this. I have a husband and three young children, high school students in need of much attention, church activities and responsibilities, and a burgeoning business with clients relying on me.

Despite my pain and inability to keep down my food, I haven't taken the time to find out what is wrong. I pass out in the middle of a conversation. "Perhaps I should make an appointment with my doctor." Months of tests and examinations, six different doctors. Zero answers.

"Mrs. Gauff, we want to do an ultrasound. Can you come in?"

The technician gets to work. When she comes to the right side of my abdomen, she is alarmed. "Oh my God; I do not know how you are still alive!" She apologizes and hurries to get the doctor.

"You have an acute case of gallbladder pancreatitis—imagine a large quarry of stones and sucking golf balls through straws," he says. I cannot. "We have never seen a case this severe in 20 years!"

I ask him, "Do you know the cause?"

"No, the best we can determine is stress. Surgery is necessary."

"I don't have time for surgery; I will think about it, and let you know."

Frustrated, he clears his throat. "Yvette, I didn't want to say this, but since you are not cooperating, I must. You are dying! And if you don't have the surgery, you won't have to worry about taking care of your students or anyone else; you won't be here to do so."

The sun shines warmly on my face as I leave. A bench across from the hospital beckons me to sit beneath the cherry blossoms. A monarch butterfly flits past me and lands on the edge of the bench, moving toward me as if coming for a chat. Butterflies are one of my favorite creatures, masters of reinvention in motion, a lesson of struggle. My little visitor stops shy of my shoulder, sitting motionless, then without provocation, flies away, leaving me with my thoughts.

"Dying? Hmph, how ironic," I think. I once desired death. The emotional pain and depression I experienced for so long led me to spend a good deal of time wanting to die; death seemed a viable answer to my problems. I had contemplated it, planned it, but never actually had enough guts to see it through. My body was giving me what I thought I had wanted. But now that it was real, as death seems imminent, it is no longer so desirable. My body's outcry is loud and clear; it is hard NOT to listen. I don't want to die; I just do not want to live like this.

I agree to the procedures. The first is unsuccessful. The second, expected to be a simple, short laparoscopic surgery, becomes problematic once they are inside and can see the severity of my condition. The small hole is insufficient to remove the large stones; a 7" incision is made. They work for hours yet the stones, like their owner, are stubborn. A third procedure is necessary.

It is said, "Life can only be understood backwards, but it must be lived forwards." I have gone from having no time to having time to think about how I have arrived at this place of deep discontent, discouragement, and despair, and time to determine my departure from it.

While recovering, I hear a whisper prompting me to look up the definition of gall:

a) something bitter or severe,
b) bitterness of spirit, to continue to cause keen irritation or bitter resentment within the mind; fester; be painful

Talk about an "Aha" moment! The words jumped off the page and pierced my soul like a hot dagger! Familiar phrases run through my mind in italicized capital letters, silently screaming: *"HOPE DEFERRED MAKES THE HEART SICK," "AS A MAN THINKETH IN HIS HEART SO IS HE."* I am clear my suppressed emotions and negative ruminations caused my condition. I am driving nails in a coffin I unconsciously built by continuing to choose others' needs over my own and not addressing my unresolved issues. Spiritually sick, my soul too needs surgical intervention. I long to be better, the suffering over, but how? Circumstances are not changing, so what can I do? I ask my Creator for a quick fix, an emotional miracle to remove the negative blocks in my psyche. Sitting in quiet, tears flowing down my face, I hear lyrics.

If you look into your heart, with a positive mind . . .

I have a deep love relationship with music. It's been my life-blood since childhood. It has kept me *alive*! The Creator often uses music to speak to me and communicate messages. I listen.

If you look into your heart, with a positive mind
Take self-inventory of your woman and your glory
Leave the bad things behind . . .

These lyrics serve as my prescription for healing, and the blueprint from which I build. Taking inventory of my thoughts and emotions, I make time to tap into my feelings and honor them. The love and care I give to others, with intention, I give to myself—first. Growing, learning, and developing a positive mindset, I correct my thinking patterns and detox my brain physically and emotionally. I die to things that don't serve me, and with gratitude, use the power of a renewed mind to create a life I love.

After my checkup today, I return to the bench to reflect. Sadly, no butterflies. Through my shirt, I trace my scar. Closing my eyes, I reimagine it, a tattoo with colorful butterfly wings on either side. I don't know that I will get it, but the thought of it evokes a smile and brings me joy.

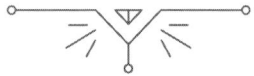

Butterfly Encounter

Dr. Janet Holliday
FLORIDA, USA

Sitting at my desk trying to focus, I can't hold a thought long enough to generate a flow of ideas. My thoughts are all over the place. I hear everything around me, the television in the other room, the air conditioner clicking on, kids outside playing, a car driving by, and someone talking to me. I grab my purse, cell phone, and journal, and it's off to my favorite spot to draft a business plan.

As I drive to the spot we refer to as the "fishing hole," I feel my body relaxing with the sun's warmth on my face, arms, and lower legs. The October air is fresh with a soft breeze. I arrive at the "fishing hole" where the kayaks and boats dock. I realize just how much my focus is off and my actions are out of cadence, creating a push energy. I have got to pull this together.

I grab a blanket from the car, a bottle of water, and my ear buds. As I walk toward the water, I notice a small area of grass with shade! I think, "Perfect." I sit on the blanket and take in the moment. I lean back, my arms and hands supporting my upper body. I look up and the sky is a perfect shade of blue with white fluffy clouds. It's super quiet. Seagulls are flying over the water;

fish are jumping in and out of the water making a splashing sound and causing a ripple effect in the water. I hear heavy breathing. A dog runs over to me, and the owner calls out, "Charlie get back over here." Charlie is smiling and wagging his tail. I see a few orange and black butterflies and I am amazed because I have not seen butterflies lately. Such a beautiful sight. I take in the view and appreciate God's artistry that surrounds me. I talk to God.

"Okay, Lord, you are always with me, and I need to know that you are present. I'm hearing that if I ask, I will receive. I am asking you to send a butterfly over here to me. I just need to know that you are here, and I can connect with you."

I sit still for a few minutes, and nothing happens. The butterflies are flying away. I spot something moving in the sand close to the water. It's a crab! I try to get up quickly without scaring it and walk towards the crab. It disappears just that quick in the sand. I remember the spot, and I turn around and hurry back to my blanket to get my phone so I can take a picture.

I turn and take two steps back toward the ocean and a butterfly flies toward me. It startles me! I tell myself, it's a butterfly. I stop, take a slow deep breath and whisper, "You heard me, thank you." I feel like a child at Christmas.

I am excited and ready to start drafting a business strategy for the new year. I think God is with me and now we can plan my next steps. The ideas are flowing freely as I write on each page. I am listening to one of my favorite songs, "Deliver Me." The singer is singing with all her heart. I put my pen down and let the words of this song marinate in my heart and soul:

He leads me beside still waters
He restoreth my soul

When you become a believer
Your spirit is made right
And sometimes, the soul doesn't get the notice
It has a hole in it
Due to things that's happened in the past
Hurt, abuse, molestation
God wants to heal the hole in your soul
God rescued me from my overthinking
He wants to restore your soul.

I open my eyes, wiping away the tears. I heard a wise woman say when your heart opens your eyes leak and my heart and soul are open. I smile as I look at my business plan draft and note that the members present are me and the highest King. I pack up my things and drive home. On the drive home, I have a renewed focus on God's ever-presence and remember to ask and accept guidance. Singing the words of the song, "Deliver Me," I am smiling on the inside and outside as I think, I had an encounter with a butterfly. A Monarch Butterfly.

Pursuing Bliss (3rd Edition)

Rose Brzezinski Lewis
MINNESOTA, USA

Here I am alone in Arizona learning the final puzzle pieces behind the mystery of 18 years of chronic pain and fatigue.

Gone is the constant headache with high sensitivity to light and sound, a horror for a professional musician. I no longer live in bed or in a recliner. I don't wait until my bladder is bursting before struggling to the bathroom. Weeping while suppressing screams is over. Resolving my 15-year-long undetected dental infection relieves those extremes.

However, life in Minnesota is restricted by mold allergies. Except in winter, I can't hike or garden. I barely have enough energy to work and cook. Music is tolerable, but not enjoyable. I am trapped indoors, unfulfilled.

Whenever traveling west of Minnesota, I am more alive and able to do what I love. I tent camp, hike for hours and miles, and enjoy music. I am desperate to move for a healthier life, but years of stress have strained my marriage. Although a doctor affirms the benefits of moving, my spouse doesn't want to.

A famous psychic suggests Phoenix. After exploring there multiple times, I make my choice. We begin the divorce process, and our relationship becomes friendlier.

Before the move, unexpected assistance seems like Divine Guidance. I find a $20 bill on an empty sidewalk in front of the courthouse right after learning I need to pay cash for fingerprinting for a teaching license. On one trip, a former music colleague calls me out of the blue and connects me to a Phoenix area school official. We meet at a coffee shop and discuss my resume and band method. I land a teaching position within weeks. I also find a lovely condo close to work, so no rush hour traffic.

My confidence grows with each blessing. I change careers, move cross-country, and end the marriage, three of life's biggest stressors.

Once in Phoenix, my luck reverses. After moving in furniture in the desert heat, despite drinking water, I crumple with nausea and faintness. I call 911. I spend two nights in the hospital for a life-threatening imbalance, and add medical debt to my stress list.

During a string of weeks with over 100°F heat, my air conditioner starts malfunctioning. The warranty expires without an effective permanent repair. I leave for work each day, worried about my dog.

Unexpected teaching obstacles like no budget, late and missing equipment/materials, technology difficulties, extra-large class sizes, little supervisor guidance, and lower than expected take home pay create severe job stress. These and more trigger sleep-ending nightmares and daytime panic attacks.

I seek stress counseling through work, but never get it. Making local friends is difficult, but I know from past recovery work to seek support from friends, family, church, and ACA, the Adult

Children of Alcoholics 12-step group. I reach out long-distance. Among others, I connect almost daily with my former spouse.

Digestive distress sends me to the emergency room twice more, increasing my debt. Then one day I taste the previous day's chili in my chicken soup. To manage a thyroid condition, I cook a special diet. That taste of chili means my thermos is harboring bacteria, continuing the fundamental cause of my chronic fatigue.

Many weeks of stress-impaired sleep with daily food poisoning uses up all my paid time off. I have to surrender my job. I am also unemployable, since daily panic attacks and sleepless nights continue. Nightmares are now about homelessness.

Why be led to Arizona only to watch my life unravel? I feel abandoned, with dwindling confidence in myself and doubts about Higher Guidance.

Sheepishly receiving food and health care assistance, I find I don't qualify for unemployment. I finally receive professional counseling and confirmation that the nightmares and panic attacks are caused by complex PTSD. I suspected this decades earlier because of many adverse childhood experiences, known as ACEs.

At a doctor's office, I meet someone from another 12-step program with my taste in music. We begin dating. I find a new, welcoming ACA group, complete a work-reeducation program, and begin making friends. They and other practitioners help me see I still have worth and assets. Even if I don't currently understand why this is happening, a Higher Intelligence does.

I take technology classes from multiple organizations to find some way into the workforce. The work program, a life-after-divorce class, and an online course introduce me to life coaching. I discover I have been doing this in my private music lessons for years.

A free acupuncture consultation brings clarity about my next big step. As I describe chest discomfort as panic, the practitioner declares, "No. That's grief." With a jolt I realize I miss my former spouse and trees, clouds and snow, my old ACA group, and spiritual community. My body is telling me I hate living in Phoenix and still love my former life.

I return to Minnesota seven and a half months after leaving and remarry. We both realize, despite challenges, our lives are much better together.

The condo sells for a small profit. I pay off my medical debts. And the complex PTSD? Several months later, the person I dated refers me to an internationally-known Phoenix traumatologist. I learn to integrate painful past experiences for greater calm and better sleep.

I rebuild my shattered life and start to pursue a long-lost childhood passion, horses. Within a year, I begin a new career as a certified life coach. Later, I add another coaching certification proven effective for relieving stress, trauma processing, and preventing burnout.

Because of the move to Phoenix, I connect with that traumatologist and discover life coaching. Even adversity has bliss to harvest: answers to mysteries, new directions, better relationships, greater trust in Divine Intelligence, and healing.

Gather adversity's harvest by showing up, seeking connections, accepting support, being open to guidance, and taking the next best steps, one at a time.

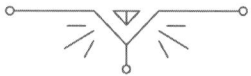

A Mother's Roar

Raquel Hernandez-Meyer
CALIFORNIA, USA

It is December 2015, and I am sitting on my sister's porch wrapped in a warm blanket, sipping a hot cup of coffee and looking out onto the tree-lined street. I stepped out to take in the warmth of the morning sun.

It has been a little over a year now that I have heard my husband say very hurtful things to me and refer to me as his ex-wife.

This morning, I am mustering up the courage to file for divorce to end 20 years of marriage.

I am swept away by a memory of my winter tradition. Winter is my time to hibernate with my family and to nest. I am feeling nostalgic for the homemade cookies, the endless Hallmark movies, the handmade ornaments, spending many weekdays in our pajamas, and the smell of cinnamon, Mexican hot chocolate, and fresh pine.

I imagine being back at home with my family, decorating our Christmas tree with the ornaments we have collected over time.

I imagine our traditional Christmas breakfast feast with all of our favorite food. We make pancakes on the tabletop electric grill. My daughter adds chocolate chips to her pancakes, walnuts and bananas for my son, and I add walnuts to mine. I cut out a round center of the bottom of the English muffin and cook an egg in the center of it and add Canadian bacon and cheddar cheese. There is a bowl of strawberries cut in half, a bowl of blueberries, and a bowl of cut-up bananas. There is a plate of crispy bacon, a plate with tamales, and a plate with scrambled eggs. There is orange juice, a carafe with coffee, and hot water for hot chocolate. And of course, we can't forget the whipped cream for the hot chocolate, the pancakes and for anything else for that matter; it's Christmas after all.

We are gathered around the table wearing our warm and comfy pajamas, smiling and excited to open up our presents.

This memory with my kids has a strong pull from the deepest part of my heart.

Just as I am feeling enveloped by the warmth of my children's expressions of love and joy, I am drawn back to the porch by the loud squawking of a bunch of colorful parakeets in flight.

I take another sip of coffee. I try to step back into that memory with my kids and instead I get a glimpse of what could be if I stay in my marriage.

I see that the cost to stay in my marriage and stop the recurring arguments with my husband is to hang my Transformational Trainer boots up for good and to admit to having an affair that I never had. I look up and see the nail on the wall at the entrance of my home calling me and tugging on my heart to hang my boots. That's all I need to do and I'm home. I take off my boots and tie up the laces to hang them up. As I begin to reach for the nail with my boots, I look over and see my kids watching as I reach out to hang them.

I can see their eyes looking at me and paying very close attention. I notice that I am teaching them what it looks like when you give up on your dreams, your passions, and that incessant tug of your soul's calling.

This reflection from their eyes stops me dead in my tracks and jolts me back to the present.

I take a deep breath, close my eyes and exhale. I begin to pray to God for support. I can't do this alone. My tears are flowing down my face. I am feverishly searching for the courage and the wisdom to make the right step. In this deep prayer, I feel a portal open within me that reaches back so far that I pass my mother, my grandmothers, and pass all their mothers before them to call in their courage to take our ancestral journey further than it has ever reached in their lifetimes.

I can feel their blessing through that courage that comes back from each of them to me, and through me with a kind of roar that only a mother can roar.

I am clear now. I understand that the memories are mine to keep alive in my heart forever. I decide to take the next bold step into a new beginning and into the next chapter of my life. I will file for divorce, and I make a promise to all my abuelas and God that I will have him served by my birthday in January.

I dry up my tears, blow my nose, and finish drinking my cup of coffee, looking out onto the tree-lined street.

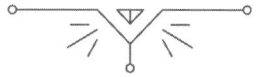

My Dark Night

Beth Beurkens
CALIFORNIA, USA

It's a late summer evening in Southern Oregon. The crickets are chirping loudly in our backyard.

Wildfires are raging to the north and east of us. I'm home alone with my beloved Golden Retriever. Our car has been packed all day. We're ready to evacuate.

Night has fallen, and I see the eerie orange glow of the fire up in the mountains.

Our house is smoky, and I've been coughing all day. I'm terrified, as people to the east of us are having to evacuate right now.

I'm in my condo in the foothills of the Siskiyou Mountains. This dry lightning fire started up on the Pacific Crest Trail above us and huge winds are fanning the flames on the tinder-dry land and the giant Ponderosa Pines up there. The wildfire is now burning out of control.

We could die here.

We could also die being trapped by downed trees and power lines if we leave. My Golden Retriever is whining and pacing in our smoky living room.

I am paralyzed with fear . . .

A horrible burning sensation of bile coats my mouth and throat.

I am holding my car keys in my hand . . . watching texts from the City of Ashland . . .

Should we stay . . . or should we leave right now? Can we still get out?

Abruptly . . . I sit down.

I remember to breathe—breathe in deeply through my nose . . . in and out . . . in and out.

And as I breathe, a cooling stillness washes over me.

A tiny voice pierces my soul . . . it says "Wake up, Beth . . . this moment is not about staying or fleeing . . . this is about a greater life that is calling to you . . . it's time to return home to friends and family and your larger work that is waiting for you in the Monterey Bay . . ."

"You've had a good life here for nine years . . . and your larger life is calling to you now . . ."

A calmness floods my whole being. I know this is a voice straight from Source . . .

I hadn't really been paying attention to what I would absolutely love in my life.

Do I really want to continue living and teaching college writing here in this valley?

It's been a good life . . . but yeah . . . it's not the greater life I feel called to.

I put my car keys down.

Just then I get a text message from the city that the wind has shifted. We don't need to evacuate.

It took being trapped in a wildfire to wake me up to the Greater Life calling to me.

And yet . . . even with this deep clarity—"I am moving back home to the Monterey Bay"—the old story and the old way of living fight like dragons to keep me from leaving.

Friends too, say, "Are you crazy, Beth? You've got the best job teaching writing at Rogue Community College. People are standing in line to get hired there."

My dean pleads with me to not leave, saying, "We'll never find anyone to replace you, Beth. I wish you'd stay. You are part of the heartbeat of the Writing Department."

Oh, this one really pulls at me, and I begin to question . . . *what am I doing?*

And there are the doubts from the property managers in Pacific Grove. "Oh, this is a really tough market, Beth. We've got the Cal State University students and the Army military families and the Defense Language Institute students. It's really hard to find anything here . . . and you've got a big dog . . ."

Internally, I'm also battling with the fear of the California prices. I'm only paying $925.00 a month now for a 3 bedroom, 2 bath, and I'm told I'll never find a California home for less than $3,000 a month.

And then there are all my friends who I am so connected with . . . my beloved poets' group and college colleagues and neighbors and dog trainers and oh, the Lake of the Woods, where we go every week, so SkyBear can swim and I can write and meditate . . . and our view of Grizzly Peak from our back yard.

So many voices and circumstances are pulling at me to stay. "Don't change." "You've got so much good here, Beth."

These are the voices of logic and common sense.

And alongside all these, is the powerful, relentless, gentle voice of my soul . . . like the ocean rolling to shore. I keep asking myself . . . but what would I love? And what if I could move? And what if it were easy?

But the money . . . the money . . .

I speak with my beloved mentor, Mary Morrissey, in our Life Mastery Gold group and she blows the lid right off my paradigm. She looks right into me and says, "God doesn't think $3,000 is big, Beth."

And I realize in that moment that three thousand dollars isn't big. The paradigm is breathing life and helium into it, so it's become huge.

Sitting in the Monterey Marriot Hotel in the Jane Fonda Room they've given to us, looking at the rental ads . . . I suddenly pause as I remember—Hey! here's a Universal Law at work here! The law of Demand and Supply.

"I'm putting my faith in the Law. There has to be a perfect home waiting for us here because I'd love it!"

I finally find the home of our dreams for $2900 a month with a partial ocean view and an enormous wrap-around deck. The owner tells me she believes I'll be an asset to the community here.

That voice of clarity that spoke to me during the wildfire has carried me all the way back home to the Monterey Bay where I am now serving my calling as a shamanic teacher, international best-selling author, and vision quest guide at a much higher level of prosperity and soul's purpose.

So, here's the thing. What if we didn't need a crisis to create something meaningful and life-changing for our lives?

If I Only Hadn't Reacted

Ivica Karas
CANADA

A sudden feeling of emptiness invades me, and I am noticing the pain in my abdomen. Were these the only words I could have used? Is this what I really wished to achieve? As I continue chopping vegetables for the evening soup for my family, thoughts of doubt, worry and despair continue to overflow.

My spouse has just left with our two children for an evening bath, and I am noticing this isn't just another of our quick-fix arguments. This time I have over-reacted by raising my voice and showing a gesture of disrespect toward her. I reacted for self-protection and out of fear.

Thoughts continue to run through me as I am left in an empty kitchen. It no longer matters that I felt treated badly just a moment ago. I no longer care who was right or wrong. I no longer worry that the family day was badly planned because of my wife's appointment, of which I didn't know, even if she had mentioned it to me. Right now, I am only noticing the feelings of self-doubt, fear and loneliness. "If I only hadn't reacted," I'm thinking.

I recall my beloved entering the door only minutes ago,

suggesting we put a calendar of our appointments on the wall. She was trying to fix the problem by placing attention on a benefit for all. I recognize this is exactly what I thought before she returned home: we needed better planning. She didn't want to hurt me, but still the blaming and victimizing took over my voice of reason and I reacted as I did.

But if I was thinking the same way she did as a way forward to help us plan our family's time, why did I react the way I did? What if "me feeling hurt" was only a part of me? What would the other part of me have thought, have felt, and have done?

I start reproducing the scene, imagining how I'm welcoming my spouse's idea as she enters the house and thanking her for thinking about the way forward. I see myself acknowledging and compassionately accepting our imperfections, now with a clear idea of how we can improve. I catch myself thinking again: If I only hadn't reacted, would this have resulted in a soothing hug or a kiss which would make us both feel strengthened and connected? Would the outcome be a precious family moment where the four of us are sitting on pillows around a dining room table, saying our gratitudes for the day around an evening candle and an inviting meal?

My children run down the stairs in PJs with still-red cheeks and damp hair after a refreshing evening bath. "Is the dinner ready?" they both cry in one voice. I watch them giggling and enjoying the soup. My face is frozen; it feels numb and a knot in my stomach reminds me of where I am. "No way I can eat right now," I'm thinking. My spouse comes down the stairs, picks an item to quickly return back to the bedroom. She doesn't wish to join us nor to eat. My seven-year-old gives me a concerned look and asks, "Why don't you eat? Are you angry?"

I continue to sit and wonder. If the part of me I was leaning on was putting all my attention on feeling defensive and resentful, what would leaning on the part of me that was all about "us" look like? Would it be all about love and compassion, knowing that we are two souls of equal light on a path of continuous growth? Now I know what leaning on me looks like and what leaning on us may have resulted in. If I only hadn't reacted, I'm thinking.

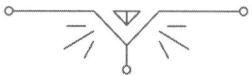

Letting Intuition Lead

Jenny Von Zastrow
MEXICO

Kenya is a beautiful East African country. Nairobi, the bustling capital, sits at 6000 feet and is a malaria-free oasis. We have been living on the city's outskirts for five years, enjoying the beauty of this wild country and its unique culture. The colors of the flowering trees, the smoky smells of open fire cooking, and the sounds of horns honking and people singing are daily occurrences.

Below its beauty, Kenya is an emerging country with a population of four out of every ten people under fifteen. There is no money to be spent on infrastructure. Traffic jams are everyday events, and carrying water, snacks, and a good book in the car is imperative. Electricity is out as often as it is on. When it returns, it usually comes on with a surge so strong it blows up anything plugged into the wall. Phone service is sketchy, to say the least, as there are no cell phones or internet. Phone lines rarely work due to the copper lines being stolen and sold by those desperate for an income.

In Kenya, medical services are no-frills, and having children here can be risky. That said, I am delighted to say that the birth of our son went well. He is a full-term baby, and we make it home from the hospital without any problems. Now that we are home, our son is finding it difficult to settle into his new life. Sleepless nights and fussy days are becoming all too familiar.

As days go by, his crying escalates. I make an appointment with the pediatrician, and off we go. Going back and forth to the doctor has become a regular occurrence. I've never been around newborns or anyone with a baby. My extended family lives half a world away, so I put my trust in the doctor and in my "motherly" intuition. As I walk into the doctor's office, he says, "Keep breast-feeding until we figure this out. There is nothing better for a baby than their mother's milk." I question my feeling that something more must be wrong, but take the doctor's advice. I return home, hoping my son will soon settle into this big world.

Within days he is passing blood in his stool. The doctor sends us to the local hospital, where they'll examine his colon with an x-ray and barium. This procedure is traumatic for my son, and challenging for me to witness. As we wait for the results, life continues with sleepless nights and non-stop crying, and I question my ability to be a mother.

We meet with the doctor again, and he explains, "I've been a doctor a long time and have seen everything. The results of the tests show that the colon is ulcerated. Your son is failing to thrive, but for now, keep doing what you are doing." To me, this is a red flag, the final straw; the most challenging words for anyone to say are "I do not know." And after months of the same advice, I feel like this doctor does not know what is wrong, yet he will not admit it.

I am scared, frustrated, and worried as I leave the doctor's office. Calling on my intuition and asking for an answer, I am inspired to call a friend in the USA. He is a doctor of tropical medicine, and although we have ruled out parasites and other tropical diseases, it feels right to get his opinion. When I finally get a clear phone connection and chat with him, he says, "I do not know what is wrong, but I feel confident that your son is not able to survive the long flights back to the USA." He suggests we go to London, which is only a little over a nine-hour flight away. A strong voice within me says, "Go!" I know it is the right thing to do.

Wasting no time, we get a life flight to London and schedule an appointment at a well-known children's hospital for exploratory surgery. When we touch down in London, my husband's colleagues meet us and graciously take us to the hospital. Arriving at the hospital, expecting to be admitted and prepared for surgery, I am told there is no bed available. Panic and frustration start to overtake me. I suppress the alarm by taking several deep breaths, and calmness rises within me. I have to trust the process. At this moment, the admitting nurse suggests another hospital, and off we go.

We arrive at the second hospital, and they put us in a room with an extra bed so I can stay with my son. They assure me a doctor will see us first thing in the morning. Wow! I feel tired yet ecstatic, knowing we are in the right place for the first time in weeks.

At daybreak, a doctor comes in and examines my son. He tells me how he recently conducted and published a study on children with allergies to milk protein found in their mother's milk. He said it is pretty rare, but my son is showing all the signs of this allergy. He suggests we postpone surgery and try taking my son off breast milk for 24 hours to see if there is a change. I am thinking, what is another 24 hours? I remind myself to trust the process.

Within minutes the nurse inserts a feeding tube into my son

and feeds him an elemental formula. Every couple of hours, a nurse shows up to check on my son and give him this formula. That night my son sleeps, and I begin to let go and relax.

The doctor returns first thing in the morning. He is pleased with the results, and we agree to continue down this path for the next week. Throughout the week, I notice significant changes; he is crying less, the ulcer in his colon has healed, and my son's weight has increased. He is happier, more curious, and has color to his cheeks. After we've been in the hospital for two weeks, my husband joins us, and we move to an apartment for another two weeks of observation. Trusting the process led us to the right doctor and place at the right time. We avoided surgery and found an answer to my son's ailment. Asking and listening made room for the right action and confirmed my belief that anything is possible.

Stepping onto the plane headed back to Kenya, holding my healthy, happy boy in my arms, a feeling of joy and gratitude rushes over me. We are returning home.

Double Rainbow

Cynthia Kuniej Berry

NEVADA, USA

The museum is a buzz of activity, as the new modern wing is under construction and the staff is occupied with preparations. I am grateful for my new internship at one of the premier art museums in the country. At the end of the year, I will have my master's degree in art conservation. Walking to our department after inspecting a large canvas in the gallery, we pass a group of art handlers moving a huge Anselm Kieffer painting. I ask my colleague, "Who is the tall guy with the red beard that looks like Vincent Van Gogh?" She says, "That's Tom, head preparator for the 20th century collection; he's a nice guy." I remember he said, "Hi!" to me this morning. Back in the studio, I continue cleaning the small Francesco Guardi on my easel. I have been training since discovering restoration in Florence while studying in Italy. My career is just taking off.

With this part of my life coming together, I can focus on my personal life. I take sailing lessons and train for a marathon. Every Sunday I pray for my family and ask God for someone to share my life with. My only requests are that this be someone I can share my faith with, and who will love my family. I trust I am heard. I have occasional dates, but no one is right for me.

The year passes. I graduate and stay at the museum on a fellowship. The modern wing opens soon. I am assigned to clean a large Sol Le Witt sculpture with the preparator, the guy with the red beard. Tom is reserved and professional; we work well together. Next week I inspect artworks in storage with a donor; Tom provides access. The day of the grand opening, I finish the survey, and staff members leave to dress for the black-tie gala. Tom asks me why I have not left, and I say that I was not invited. Surprised, he asks if I will go with him. Hesitant, I agree to meet at the staff entrance in a couple of hours.

I have the perfect black dress from a vintage shop. I slip into it and some heels. Walking into the museum, I feel radiant, and Tom looks smart in his tuxedo. At the entrance, floral arrangements stretch toward the ceiling, and music floats through the corridors. Colleagues nod to see me with Tom. I am smiling. A camera flashes, capturing the moment. As we tour the galleries, Tom is informed and enthusiastic, telling me about the art he installed. When he drives me home, Tom kisses me, and I realize what a magical time this spontaneous evening has been.

I invite Tom to an exhibit, and friends are happy to see us together. We take lunches in the park outside the museum. We spend all our free time together. As we walk home one evening, Tom tells me he loves me, and we look up to see a double rainbow over the lake. I tell him that I love him too. My sister calls one evening and he is interested in knowing about my family. We learn we are both from large, close families. Soon after, I am stunned when Tom asks me to move in with him. I've never lived with a guy before, yet this seems a natural thing. It is not a decision I take lightly. We find an apartment we love. Tom shares Thanksgiving with my family, and they like him. He invites me to meet his family at Christmas. Up until now, I never thought about marriage. This feels right. He does not ask me. In fact, things are now off between us; Tom is withdrawn. By springtime, he moves out of state to go back to school. I cannot believe this is happening to me!

Tom asks me to trust and says he will stay connected. I am hurt that he writes, but is unreceptive on the phone. Devastated, I cannot understand. He tells me to be strong. I decide to get help and do considerable soul searching and reading. I realize I am co-dependent. I do not want to spend the best years of my life waiting for someone who does not want to be in a permanent, loving relationship with me. I need to let go.

Uninterested, I date other people for distraction. I take classes and train for another marathon. To my surprise, Tom starts calling me. Because I worked hard to regain independence, I do not accept his calls. I cannot be hurt again. Now aware of Tom's weaknesses, I decide not to see him again. My family and friends are happy I am over Tom and stronger. He persists calling. In a moment of weakness, I accept his call, and he asks to visit. It is time for a ten-minute sweaty conversation. When we meet, I notice things in him I never saw before. I am objective and indifferent.

It is my birthday, and it is drizzling. We go for a run on the lakefront. Tom explains himself. I am angry and tell him why I do not want to continue our relationship. He tells me that he loves me and cannot live without me, and says, "That is why I want to live the rest of my life with you." I cannot believe his audacity! Now, I am supposed to trust him? I do not recognize his proposal and get a headache. At my apartment he asks me to marry him and explains what he sees for us in the future. I am considering his proposal. Tom says that he will wait for an answer because he knows that it will take me time. I know I have always loved him, and cannot run from true love, the man God chose for me. We meet my mom the next day and she says, "You two will be fine!" She knows Tom is sincere and loves me.

Our wedding is May 11th, my late father's birthday. I know my dad would have loved Tom and they would have gotten along. Looking at the photo taken thirty-five years ago on our first date, I am happy I listened to the still small voice that said, "trust." I trusted God for my perfect life partner. I trusted myself to grow, and trusted Tom's love. That year apart helped us become stronger and more committed to our love. After experiencing joy and struggles, tragedy and loss, countless blessings, and challenging work on our relationship, we still enjoy sharing our one life. We decide to trust our love together every day.

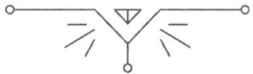

Empty Nester to Changing Lives

Young Csernus Young
CALIFORNIA, USA

It is a nice fall day with some autumn colors to give us a taste of fall here in California. We are back from Colorado.

There is so much mail to open! We are so excited for our youngest daughter. She is moving to Denver for a culinary management training program at the magnificent Gaylord Resort. Our oldest got married in August and our youngest will be gone in a short month. Our eldest's wedding was everything she dreamed of. We were in the middle of huge pine trees with a picture-perfect outdoor ceremony. It is such an odd feeling to think how my job as a mother in some ways is complete. Just like that, in a twinkling of an eye, my daughters transformed into young, independent women. I am not sure what way they will need me now. This is the start of the empty nester era. Being a mom has been the most important job I have had. Okay, okay, back to focusing on the mail.

I pick up an envelope, the result of my recent mammogram. I am staring at the letter; it states that they want to repeat it. An alarm is going off in me. My mom is a breast cancer survivor. Can it be, no it cannot be? I am pushing the thought away. I am making the decision not to think the worst and to keep it to myself. Christmas is right around the corner; then we are helping my daughter to move. I schedule my 3D mammogram at the beginning of the next year.

We are on the way home from Colorado.

I am looking at my new result. There is a small mass in my breast. Should I panic? How should I feel? I have different thoughts racing through my mind. I brush them away. The next step is a biopsy. A realization hits me. I am just like my mom. I am protecting the people closest to me from worrying.

I am hosting four high-school girls from China for a week. Wait, my other two groups are canceling due to a mysterious virus.

My parents keep asking me to visit. With no students, I hop on a plane to Hungary. It is so nice to be home! Today is a retro disco night with my cousins. I am sightseeing with my tour guide friend in Budapest over the weekend and connecting with a special friend.

I am ready to burst at the seams. I have been pushing away my thoughts about my upcoming biopsy and what it could mean. I am pouring my heart out to my closest childhood friends. Main pieces of advice: Do not have surgery! Think holistic healing! Change how I think and eat! Watch miraculous healing journeys!

Do you know what is crazy? The coronavirus is everywhere now. I have a confirmed trip to fly back. The airports everywhere are very eerie; there is a ghost-like emptiness, and on the planes, rows and rows of empty seats.

I am ready to learn the truth. It is biopsy time! My mind is wandering, it was hard being so far away when my mom was going through cancer treatments. My heart ached for her. Okay, okay, this story is about my journey. My heart is beating faster. I hear at the appointment after the biopsy that there is no cancer. Yeah! A wave of emotions washes over me. Wait, he is talking about surgery to remove a group of atypical cells, to take out a golf-ball size mass from my breast to be safe, for real? There is a 20/80% chance of these abnormal cells becoming cancer. My still small voice says no. I am weighing my options. I have a date for surgery. The doctor is not very happy about answering my million questions.

Today I seek advice about my decision from other Hungarian friends. I hope to quiet that voice within me. The voice gets louder. My friends are on the same wavelength as me. The doctor is surprised by my cancellation. He orders an MRI. It is not exactly fun. He is not afraid to show his frustration. He surprises me when he tells me if I were his wife, I would have had this surgery, or that difficult patients like me are back in a year with cancer. He avoids answering my questions about how changing my diet and lifestyle could work. I know this, he will not be my doctor anymore.

I am making drastic changes in the way I eat and live, switching to a plant-based diet. I juice and make green smoothies daily. I am learning a lot about food that fights and prevents cancer. We moms take care of others, but do not always take care of ourselves. The past 14 years have been stressful and difficult. My husband was diagnosed with epilepsy. It has been a crazy roller coaster ever since.

The first things I noticed were the physical changes in me. My mind cleared up in such an amazing way! I always heard that when you eat clean, your mind gets uncluttered, but to experience it! It is out of this world! I am reading and watching everything I can put my hands on about people who cured themselves of diseases just by lifestyle change. I am fascinated with this subject.

It's been six months and I am holding my recent mammogram

result in my hand, opening it slowly . . . and it is NEGATIVE. Do you hear me? It is *negative*. I did not have surgery, but you know what I did do. I believe that this journey of prevention will clear out the atypical cells and I will be just fine. I chose a path that was not popular with my doctor. I do understand that the changes I made must be lifelong. I am imagining myself healthy and staying healthy with my new lifestyle.

You can be sure of one thing. I am sharing my little miracle of transformation with everyone I encounter on my path and trying to inspire people to do the same. My girlfriend looked at me one day and asked: Have you ever thought of becoming a life coach? I found my calling through this health journey. I am now a certified life coach.

You are never too old for change, or to fall in love with a life you love living. We are more willing to change when we face big challenges and stick with a new way of thinking. What will it take for you to take a step towards a new you, a life you love?

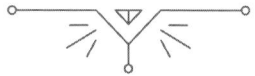

Awaken Your Light

Sherry Ann Bruckner, JD

MINNESOTA, USA

Looking at the Austin skyline, his voice breaks the silence. "That's the Capitol off to the right and to the left is . . ." Similar name-tags on our blue neck lanyards show us both as law conference attendees.

He asks me to join him for dinner. I accept. Our meal passes quickly. We stroll the city, remaining nearly inseparable the rest of the conference.

Although 700 miles separate our homes, we plan to see each other again soon. Instead of typical local dates of occasional dinners and movies, we connect for long weekends of exploring and hand-holding, which I quickly begin referring to as "vacation dating."

During a trip to my home, AJ asks if I am willing to relocate to Austin. I feel both excitement—"Could he be the one?" and fear—"Oh, wait, moving for a guy I just met?" I tell him it is too soon for me to think about that.

Our Fourth of July vacation date weekend begins with hiking, laughing, and enjoying majestic mountain views. As we sit at dinner, AJ leans in and quietly says he has something to tell me.

His next words hit my ears like a foreign language that I barely comprehend. "I'm married," he whispers.

My mind stops. It fails to even muster the racing thoughts of, "What? How could that be? What the . . ." and instead swirls with emptiness. Shock and silence. Now grateful the chair supports my suddenly lead-filled body, I sit with the proverbial jaw drop for what seems like an eternity. If hearts sink, mine takes a 14,000-foot torpedo plunge into the Pacific Ocean. His words, "We live apart and are going to get a divorce," drift off.

Before I leave the table, I ask why he said nothing sooner. His response is, "You never would date me." Well, it seems that AJ knows me. I feel disappointment in not knowing him.

Could this be the same guy seemingly so kind, gentle, respectful, generous, and genuine? The pain and grief of losing what I see as a flourishing love and the utter shame of being so wrong in this instance seems almost too much.

What have I done? Wait, didn't he ask me months ago about moving to Austin?

I quietly exit the restaurant alone. Somehow my body carries my broken heart and shame-filled head back to the cabin. Although it feels like a treacherous walk, it simultaneously seems something carries me before the tears gush and the deep sobbing consumes my body. My drenched face projects a combination of pain and shame and grief.

How did I not know?

How could I have known?

I consider myself smart. I am a lawyer. I know better. I routinely run criminal background checks on guys before dating.

I never do a marriage check.

As he drops me at the airport, I feel like I am looking at a stranger. Days before our eyes connected in joyful smiles. Now, they bear only sadness.

My flight from Denver to Minneapolis passes with steady, quietly streaming tears. I imagine the people in the seats around me thinking someone died. A part of me did.

While I grieve the end of a relationship, I also mourn the loss of my attachment to my own innocence.

It challenges me to really question me.

Clearly, there is a type of person who dates a married person, and certainly that was not me. Yet his words, "I'm married," transform me into that woman in this one time and place. I've been so careful about dating, often accused of being too careful, too hesitant, too reserved. I really think I am smarter than that. No longer any smarter, and never any better, here I sit with me in all of my fallibility.

In striving for perfection, and expecting perfection, I lose my connection to my own self.

The break proves necessary.

The breaking open of me and the attachments that do not serve me or anyone around me.

As I release judgments about what type of people do what types of things, I embrace the fullness of my own humanity.

I see that carrying hurt and distrust hinders me. My ideas about the way things are supposed to be prevent me from appreciating, acknowledging, and fully enjoying and experiencing what is.

Being so sure about what it means to be good or bad, I collide head-on with the reality that I am both.

As my heart cracks again, a little more light reveals itself.

Do I hide it, or let it free?

Memories invite compassion and joy or shame and pain.

I may choose which invitation to accept.
One serves me and the people around me.
The other serves no one.
One invites me to awaken my light.
I accept the invitation to awaken my own light.
It is time to shine.

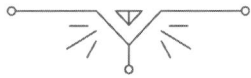

Notice What I am Noticing

Ellen T. Reed

TEXAS, USA

Ever since I learned I was Aspie, a woman who can live independently, communicates well, and does not experience intellectual difficulties, I realized while it was euphoric to understand who I am, it is a double-edged sword. I have become so aware of why people have trouble with us, and not for a good reason; they have preconceived ideas of what being autistic is and are not willing to budge on their beliefs. This means that I will receive the effects of the limits they put on people they believe are "disabled." Disability does not enter my mind when I consider my diagnosis. I understand I am different and see the world in a more profound, more analytical way, but "disabled"? No, I am not disabled. I feel that, in many ways, I could see into people's eyes and see when they are disingenuous in what they say to me. They could tell me they are happy to see me, but their bodies are looking for an escape route.

Being Aspie, I can see all the opportunities to improve our world, as I can see issues that can be improved for the good of all humanity. Unfortunately, on the other side of the sword, these problems and conditions are found due to an experience that has caused great pain either emotionally and or physically. The Aspie woman is not a woman who will let go of the situation; she will go into hyper-focus analyzing the problem. We are women in action, never allowing a situation to continue if someone is mistreated.

Throughout my life, I have been a devout rule follower, and when someone believes that they can skirt the rules for personal gain, I am at my angriest. We serve the needs of everyone, not just the people directly impacted by someone who believes they are superior to others. I first noticed this during a childhood game of Four Squares in elementary school in which some students thought it was okay to cut the line. While it bothered me, I could also see how others were affected by this behavior.

Many people believe that our communication skills are weak, and that we show no empathy for the feelings of others. While this may be true of those who have been shut off by controlling family and society members, I believe this trait to be inaccurate. In our case, many are not shy about communicating what is appropriate. We see unethical or inappropriate behaviors or issues that can lead society in the wrong direction. Although some might call us whistleblowers, I would call us the analyzers instead. When we appear mute, we are taking in the entire scene to propose a solution to those needing to make the changes. Sometimes, if we are put on the spot to give feedback, we may stumble over words, so we are brushed off as being below the community standards, but we are proposing ideas that never occurred to those who consider us disabled.

In my interview and work experiences, I have come to notice that so many do not understand that there are women who are at the strong end of the spectrum. When we mention a diagnosis, the interviewer or colleagues automatically think that the first altercation will melt us into a tailspin. The interviewer turns off their ears, believing we are not a good fit for the company. If they gave us a chance, they would see that we are great project managers who will head off issues before they start. We are capable women ready to improve their business flow, but they have already decided we are disabled.

Another area where the sword is quite sharp is in the relationship world. In fact, as part of my published book, under my assumed name Ellen T. Reed, I express my significant concerns about men who do not look closely enough at a woman's heart before discarding her for "not being their type." This is a case of men looking at our exterior shell and deciding if we will make their insecure hearts look better when we are around. Unfortunately, when some men marry, they learn shortly after the marriage of the "beautiful couple" that they are headed for divorce, as they never knew to look at the heart, too. They never learned where their shared interests lay; it only mattered what she looked like. I had experienced a different scenario; I was falsely shown admiration to cover his sexual insecurity. Others may be deceived by recently widowed men or those looking for a side hustle. They believe we will never notice the truth, but we certainly do, and not until after we are trapped.

The last place that we need assistance is in receiving resources. Many people are surprised when we say we are late-diagnosed with Aspies. They ask, "Didn't they know in school that you needed so much more help than you received?" We get tired of telling those that look incredulously at us that we flew under all the red flags. Many of us received high grades, so the belief was that we were female nerds. We were not having behavioral issues as we sat quietly in the corner or on the playground with our noses in a book. The only place that indicated our troubles was gym class, when we were always picked last. All we received was a pass to the guidance counselor for emotional assistance. However, now that we are in the adult world competing with our colleagues, plenty of services need to be set up for us to receive a level playing field of opportunities. The first service is to educate those who do not understand our vast capabilities. Other areas include employment opportunities that utilize our skills, affordable housing, and legitimate financial and legal protection assistance from scams and identity theft.

Considering all that I have noticed in my three years of study, my acute understanding of my needs will have me go to all lengths to help all of us Aspies receive the resources to live the lives we deserve. As a coach, I will use my pains to analyze issues, create possibilities, educate society members who still believe we are disabled, and then find solutions, so we all live better lives. I noticed our life, and I refuse to let us continue in substandard ways. I will take every action wherever necessary to help us rise above the negative stigmas.

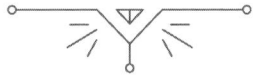

Press Pause on Panic

Maggie Everett
UNITED KINGDOM

The phone rang and, as I looked at the screen, I saw it was my chair of trustees. "That's strange," I think, as I reach for it. Not only was it out of our normal working hours, but we had only just exchanged emails an hour or so ago about the sessions we were running at the conference in a couple of days.

"I am so sorry Maggie," he says, "but I am afraid we have received a serious complaint about you. We have just held an emergency trustees' meeting and, following legal advice we have been given, we are suspending you from your role until we have conducted an independent review of the allegation."

I went cold . . . sorry . . . *what*?

What on earth had I done? How had I managed to upset someone that much that they had complained about me to my trustees? My brain kept whirling, trying to think of possibilities, and came up with nothing that could warrant such an action. Who was accusing me and of what?

I was informed that I was not allowed to know what the allegation is, who had lodged the complaint or what had happened, until

I'd spoken with the independent investigator. This was to be the next person to contact me.

I sat, frozen in place, and true enough, the next call was from Sarah, representing the Human Resources company whose advice my trustees had sought. "You have allegedly made racist and defamatory remarks in the public domain. There will be an independent examination of the allegation which will include an interview with you at the end of the week, to which you are entitled to bring someone. I will be sending you a summary of the allegation, and you are not to speak with anyone about this."

There were other comments, but these wash over me as yet again my mind runs on overdrive, searching for answers: How on earth can this have happened and who could have made that allegation? I know we all possess unconscious bias, but . . . racist? And inflammatory?

I want to cry, but no tears will fall . . . I feel like screaming but nothing comes out . . . I am shivering, shaking as if it was freezing cold but the room remains warm. How? What? Who?

Remembering the "press pause on panic" Brave Thinking tool I had learned, I make an appointment to talk to the fear. (I will lose my job, no one will ever trust me again, I must be a really awful person, who has got it in for me?) in three days' time (that would be Thursday evening, the day before my appointment with the investigator). Then I take a sheet of paper, and I start to think of what good can be found in this situation. Good? In this? Well, if nothing is bad unless we say it is, I guess there must be some good in it somehow.

I suppose I don't have to travel to London now in the middle of February; I have my session notes and recordings so someone else can use them; I can take some time out and do what I like.

Refusing to entertain the millions of negative thoughts trying to invade my mind, I focus on reading and listening to positive mindset recordings and asking God to speak to me as I drop off to sleep.

I wake in the early hours of the morning. My thoughts immediately go to what had happened a few hours earlier. I speak to the Universe, the cat (and myself!): "I am NOT going to give in to this." I pick up my phone and look up a Bible verse for the day and read:

"The Lord will fight for you. Just stay calm."

As I reflect on this situation two years later, I know that pressing pause on panic works. Yes, I had a few wobbles, moments of self-doubt and anxiety, but looking for the positive and what I could find to be grateful for in the situation helped me change my focus. It started a deeper engagement with looking for the positive, finding it is possible to be grateful in every situation, and perhaps most importantly has enabled me to realize I am connected with a power and source which is far greater than I and which has a solution for every situation.

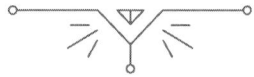

Shine Your Light

Mandy Morris

AUSTRALIA

As a young girl, I said to my mum, "The only time I ever felt truly *on* was when I was on stage." I was shy and lacking in confidence. Being on stage somehow gave me permission to shine my light and connect deeply with others. Connection is a recurring theme in my life. I'm a walking contradiction. An Extraverted Introvert. Holder of two Ph.D.s, one in connection and the other in isolation.

My preference is the first. It embraces my creativity and celebrates my power.

Ever since I can remember, the creative arts have shown me the way home to my true nature. Creativity is my Soul food. My *on* switch. Unfortunately the switch doesn't seem to be connected. Someone, namely me, has turned off the power again!

So you find me sitting here at my desk blindly staring out the window. Nothing seems to be flowing. I've been trying to force words onto the page prematurely, hoping that through sheer effort this short story will magically reveal itself. I want it to make a difference in the lives of its readers. I want them to know that every one of them is a unique and glorious soul. That we are all creative and need to play more.

The truth is, my writing is not going well. My creative juices refuse to cooperate. They don't like being pushed. I am trying too hard, forcing my offering rather than trusting in the process. So I take a breath, in through the nose and out through the mouth. I bring to mind something I am grateful for. A beautiful spring day, my teenage son. I feel the shift immediately and the sweet relief that accompanies it. From this place, I can let go of how this story will unfold and relax into the knowing that it will.

That done, I invite my artist self to join me. I've missed her. She is my greatest teacher. Her playfulness is my superpower. I love and appreciate her innocence and spontaneity.

With her, by my side, I am Wonder Woman. I look out my window again as if for the first time. My *on* switch is now well and truly reconnected.

Everywhere I look I see the extraordinary in the ordinary. I notice the beauty of my wild unmanicured garden. I marvel at the diverse palette of greens. My triffid bougainvillaea boasts bright purple flowers, adding contrast to the canvas in front of me. Other elements vie for my attention. Weeds sprouting in clumps offer up playful violet posies just for me. One plant has even taken to growing horizontally to get my attention, like a small child learning to ride a bike shouting, "Look at me, Mum!" A rich collage of Australian bird song adds a further dimension to the visual splendor. My very own private concert is inspiring my story to unfold naturally this time. Much of my essence is reflected in this scape. The wild colorful creative. A woman wanting to share her unique flavor. To embrace her authenticity and add value. As my focus shifts, I notice with slight amusement that my desk is in complete chaos. It's covered in clutter, a word inherited from my Nana, whose shapely English legs rivalled the finest porcelain.

My eyes are drawn not to the half-drunk cold cup of coffee or the stack of notes I haven't bothered to put away but to a humble leaf.

It takes pride of place on my desk, now safely housed in a frame. It is the keeper of a precious story. A treasured moment in time. This leaf was scooped up by my then 10-year-old son as we stood by the Bodhi Tree (Buddha's Place of enlightenment) in Bodh Gaya. As if on cue, given by the smiling monk who had joined us, said leaf floated gently to the ground. It landed at my son's feet. The rest of the ground was bare. The monk gestured for him to take it. A precious gift from India. And a great travel story.

I love the power of the story. How it celebrates our humanness and connects us more deeply to each other. I've been blessed to be a Playback Theatre Actor for over 20 years. This sacred form of expression has given me a way to share and connect wholeheartedly. It has gifted me a place to stand in my greatness and be of service. Playback is improvisational theatre at its best. It's all about heart and honoring true life experiences. During a Playback performance, the audience is invited to share stories from their lives. These moments are then acted out spontaneously in drama, movement and music. I've had the privilege of playing back hundreds of people's stories. There have been laughter, tears and everything in between. On a personal level, I've experienced much of my own life played back to me by my fellow performers. This is how we rehearse. Stories of childbirth, heartbreak, India, loneliness and death, to name a few.

Playback has enriched my life on so many levels, and it holds a special place in my heart. Unfortunately, I haven't had much opportunity to perform in the last few years. I have been exploring, however, putting myself on stage imaginarily and reconnecting to the qualities I inhabit there. Bringing the wisdom of my creative self into my everyday world.

I invite you to join me on stage for a moment and experience it for yourself. I know it's a big ask, but you can do it. It's time to step out of your comfort zone and experience your fullness. The theatre lights greet you like old friends welcoming you back. You are a sunflower enjoying the warm glow. Your heart radiates love.

You stand there open and receptive, your bare feet at home on its well-worn surface. Now softly gaze out into the audience. No need to be scared. They are perfectly imperfect humans just like you. Trust. I promise you it will be all right. Besides, you are not alone. You are part of an ensemble of actors. A sacred team. You might even have fun. At last, the moment has come. You are listening deeply with your whole body. It is time to trust in the void and step forward as you play back the story told to you by the audience member. As if by magic you are in the flow, doing what you were born for. Living your purpose and sharing your light.

Deep gratitude fills your heart as you realize you have found your *on* switch.

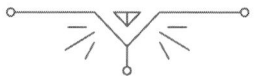

It Starts with a YES!

Luz Angélica Torres
CALIFORNIA, USA

I am sitting in a self-care workshop sponsored by my job. I am thinking to myself, "Here we go again! Someone talking about self-care, but not enough time to do it." Surprisingly, the presenter, Jennifer, starts talking about a concept I've never heard before—the power of five minutes. She shares how easy it is to destress and rejuvenate in this short period of time, and I am intrigued. Now my thoughts are, "Hmm, this sounds interesting, but really? Five minutes?" I continue listening and become more engaged with the workshop. I look around, and to my surprise, others are engaged as well. I look at how Jennifer is glowing and is so full of life, and I think, "Wow, this lady actually looks like she practices what she is talking about. I want some of that!"

Through the presentation, we are encouraged to fully participate in a movement exercise. We are paired up with a partner and decide who will be number one and who will be number two. Jennifer goes on to explain she will play a song and one partner at a time will mirror the other's movements while dancing, and then we will switch. Next, the number ones are asked to raise their hands and Jennifer says, "Okay, number twos, you are going to go first." Everyone bursts into laughter, and it eases any hesitations we are having about dancing in that moment. "Shake It Off" by Taylor Swift starts playing, and we all start shaking it off. When the exercise is over, Jennifer asks how we are feeling and everyone is sharing how much happier, lighter and more alive they feel. I think to myself, "And this was in just five minutes! I can do this!"

Toward the end of the workshop, Jennifer invites everyone present to sign up for a personal conversation with her, and as a bonus, the first 20 people who sign up will receive her 28-day program on how to start your day. I tell myself, "Luz, you have to be one of those 20 people!" It is clear to me now that I want to know more about self-care, "Jennifer style." I walk really fast to the back table, and I do it! I become the first one to sign up for a personal conversation with Jennifer.

The day of my appointment is here! I am not sure what to expect when I get on our video call. We first say hello, chit-chat about our days, and then Jennifer asks me to share about me. I share about how stressful work is, where I live, my age, and that I am a single mom of the most amazing 15-year-old son, Daniel. As we continue talking, the conversation deepens. Questions about who I am, what I like, what I do for fun, etc. unnerve me. I realize that my superficial answers make it difficult to be honest with myself. I tell her, "I can tell you the answers to these questions about Daniel, but I do not know what the answers are for me." This response makes me realize that my life is being defined not by who I am, but by my role as a mother.

At this time, Jennifer invites me to grab a piece of paper and draw a vertical and horizontal line, making a cross down the middle of the page. She instructs me to write these four categories—Health and Well-being, Relationships, Vocation, and Time and Money Freedom—one on each quadrant. Next, she asks me to write down my wishes and desires for each category without editing or worrying about how I could obtain or do these things. While I write, she walks me through a visualization of what my life could be like if money, age, gender, time, etc. were not factors. I describe what I am seeing, feeling, hearing, touching, and speaking, and she reflects my vision back to me. My heart is filled with a vision of possibilities that up until this moment had seemed out of reach. This is the first time I am aware that I am more than just a mom and that there is a different way of living and experiencing my life.

Jennifer continues the conversation by explaining the power of decision and how planting your stake in the ground helps you to claim your spot in life, so you can live a life you absolutely love. She presents an opportunity to work with her one-on-one for six months and to attend a transformational retreat in Tulum, Mexico to deepen my self-love and acceptance. "Wow, this sounds like a great opportunity, and I would love to do this, *but* . . . I have no money," I tell Jennifer, along with many other excuses. We talk about limiting beliefs and fear. Fear, I learn, is the number one killer of dreams, and I realize that my limiting beliefs are dissuading me from saying yes to mine.

My son walks in the room and I immediately share my realizations with him, and I add, "Daniel, here lies this great opportunity in front of me to travel alone and do something I have never done for myself, but it scares me, and I am not sure I can come up with the money." My son turns to me and urges, "Mom, if I asked you for the same investment to do this retreat and work with a coach, would you give me the money?" I say, "Yes! In a heartbeat." He looks me in the eye and says, "Then why can't you invest like this in yourself? You deserve it, Mom. Do it!"

I turn back to Jennifer and say, "Okay, I am ready. I am planting my stake in the ground, and I am deciding to say *yes* and invest in *me*! I don't know how this all will work out, but I know it starts with a *yes*!"

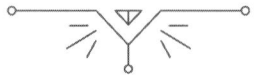

Regret is a Liar!

Lee Buckley
AUSTRALIA

A wave of emotion comes over me while contemplating the thought that Mum will die one day. Regret begins its work. Through many tears, and an occasional sob from the depth of my heart, I speak to her. "I don't want you to die, I don't want you to leave me!" With her arms around me, in her calm, soothing voice of compassion, she replies "You know I don't want to die either, sweetheart. Although it will happen one day. Let's hope it's a long way away."

Coming up to Christmas 2008, Mum phoned me with her test results: Multiple Myeloma, blood cancer! I could not get to her quickly enough. It was long day of emotions, torn between our family visiting from England and getting to my mother to hold and comfort her.

I drove the two-hour journey alone up the mountains to her. Time to cry my sadness and distress with the anticipation of what lay ahead. This was a nightmare and I wanted to wake up. I felt scared and full of disbelief. Could this really be happening?

The moment we locked eyes across the hospital ward, tears flowed from both of us. I rushed into her outstretched arms; we remained there for the longest time. I wanted to hold her and never let her go. We talked, wept, laughed and cried; our emotions were raw and vulnerable.

My sister moved in with Mum around that time and became her carer, to help her with appointments and be her support when she needed it. I am so grateful to her for being with Mum. Mum and I speak on the phone most days. On some weekends I can help too, so my sister can take time for herself.

As the days and weeks pass, the prognosis given is six to eight years. With joy we are all grateful for the time, grasping those years with both hands. We are hopeful and believe she has the time to do what she wants and leave the legacy she desires.

Alone with my thoughts, my inner critic's voice of regret continues its not-so-subtle badgering of all I am not and of everyone I let down. I wish I could be with Mum more, help more, support my sister more. On the other hand, I can justify all my decisions as to why not. A full-time job, a husband and family routine, she lives a long way from me. Besides, the prognosis is six to eight years—we have time!

This is the thing, the cancer turned out to be far more aggressive than any of us could anticipate. Kidney failure requires dialysis three times a week; there is a heart condition and finally a contagious infection. This means wearing protective gear to visit her.

We are normally an affectionate family, but I cannot even touch her, devastating for me. I just want to hug my mum! As I watch her leaving me a little more each day, I feel desperate for more time. I am not ready to let her go.

Easter time comes and my brother arrives from interstate. Mum finally has all four of her children and two sons-in-law together with her. She is unable to interact with us, but we spend time together with her. We share stories of our lives and what our children are doing now, bonding as a family again and surrounding the room with love for Mum and each other. I feel overjoyed for her. Her greatest happiness is to always have all the family together talking and laughing. These are memories I treasure still.

After that visit I stated aloud to no one in particular "It's okay if I'm not with Mum when she dies as long as someone is with her." I knew she would go soon, but I did the oddest thing. At 6:30 PM on the Friday after Easter, I turned my mobile off to charge it. This action and its consequences are now powerful ammunition for regret. I just do not know why I did that!

At 7:30 PM the hospital called my sister to say it would not be long. She then called me, and called and called and called and called! She did not have my husband's number with her. Later, regret is yelling at me, while I feel so bad for my sister because what was worse for her is Mum was asking for me and I was not there!

I am not there for Mum. I am not there for my sister. I am just not there because I turned my stupid phone off! Mum went to God that night in April, 2009.

I replay that evening over and over in my head with the voice of regret being the loudest. It constantly tells me "I cannot be trusted, I am not dependable, I do not think of anyone but myself!" The inner critic is relentless. Regret can hit us hardest at a death, with no more time, no more opportunities to say or do or change anything.

My inner critic reminds me of its catchphrases: "I should have done this . . ." "I should have said that . . ." "If only . . ." Yes, you are right! Of course, I should have said more, been more, done more, but I did not. In truth, there is no judgment, only facts.

As I think about the feeling of regret, I realize it is what I feel about the past. The past I cannot change, and still there is a temptation to dwell in the past. Not upon happy memories of an event, a gathering, or a holiday. No, I could dwell in the dark places of the past to try to fix it by remembering and rehearsing the pain. I could even consider moving in, set up house in the dark places, because it is what I know, because it feels safe, but regret is a liar.

Regret is for a brief time, not a lifetime! I allow regret to have its say, only for a moment, because the truth is it steals my time and my joy.

Now, I drown out the inner critics' version of events with love and gratitude!

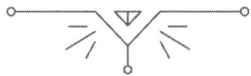

Worthy of Growth

Tracey Igoe

IRELAND

My thoughts are working me up so much that my body is contracting. I have a pain in my chest; I feel it from my heart up to my neck. My throat is so painful. I can feel my vocal cords are all twisted and knotted up. I feel unable to speak. My new delicate dream is fragile. Sharing with another person is scary.

I have been getting signs and signals from the Universe. These prompts are coming day and night. I wake up with an urge to sign up for a miniature course, one that accompanies a book I am reading. The course investment is small, but I have to check my account. I have the required amount, which is a positive sign.

I download the course workbook and start answering the questions. My answers are taking me onto a new path, a different career. I am intrigued. I do some research and go back to bed. I feel longing and at the same time many questions. Can someone like me, who left school early, become a "professional" life coach? Where can I learn this? Will learning take me from my family and business? What will it cost?

This longing will not leave me. I find a life-coach training that will take place just forty minutes from home. It starts in the spring and is one weekend a month for seven months. It sounds possible to me. I read all the details. I am getting more excited and drawn in by my fantasy and longing. I have known there is *more* to me. It has been keeping me awake at night for several months.

I have some answers, but I have some fears as well. I'm afraid of other people's judgment. Will they say, "Who does she think she is?" "Why does she want to do that?" "Isn't she all right as she is?" The pull to the *more* is greater, and I make the decision. I am going to take action and follow this calling.

Tonight is the deadline to receive a substantial early-bird discount. I have commitments. I run a bakery business from home. I have two children, a husband who works long hours, and a home to look after. I *want* to do this. I need help from my husband to pay the deposit. I know I will sort something out later to cover the monthly payments. I don't know *how* but I know I *will*. I am determined to do whatever it takes.

I have worked myself up into such a state I am afraid my voice will not work. I have just given my hubby his dinner. He is home late. He is telling me all about his day. I am thinking what I will say. I am being inspired to do something different from what I have been doing. I have a yearning to follow my inner being. He will think I am crazy if I tell him this. Up until now, he is a matter-of-fact, black-and-white type of guy. I have to explore these feelings I have. There is something inside ME wanting ME to grow.

It is past 11 PM. I feel like I will die inside if I do not speak my truth. I manage to get the words out that have been choking me all evening.

My husband is supportive and says we will make it work. We will sort something out. He does not need to know or understand what it is. Once I know myself, he will support me. He transfers some money to me. I am straight online, signing up to become a professional life coach. Putting my name down for this feels so expansive and self-validating. I am signed up. I have no idea how I'll manage everything and the monthly payments. I am experiencing the accuracy in the following quote.

> *At the moment of commitment, the*
> *Universe conspires to assist you.*
> —JOHANN WOLFGANG VON GOETHE

I commit and all sorts of help and resources come to my aid. There are lots of happy coincidences that make everything possible. I am certain that I am on the right track. This is my first time investing time and money in myself. Growth for me that will benefit many over time. This is just the beginning and . . .

I am *so* worth it.

Climbing the Slope of Thought

Maeve Lankford
IRELAND

I have had what I refer to as a "dormant dream" for over 20 years. To climb Ireland's highest mountain! As a kid, when perhaps it was more realizable, it held no interest. But when my husband and I return to Ireland in our thirties, I discover a walking group in our village that climbs Carrauntoohil annually, usually as a fundraiser for a local good cause. I see them out walking and preparing for the climb and every time I think "I'd love that."

Roll on 20 years, two careers, three wonderful boys and a worldwide pandemic and here I am still thinking "I'd love that." And I'm finding myself further from its possibility than ever— overweight, unfit and crippled after a 12-kilometre hike.

I go to see a physiotherapist because I'm so sick of feeling like this. I'm only 52, for heaven's sake! He's unimpressed with my wallowing and to a certain extent with my degree of unfitness, but he tells me what I need to hear. "Whether you climb Carrauntoohil or not, Maeve, you should be able to climb it! You're too young to settle for anything less." We agree on that and I determine to make myself able for it.

And so begins the journey to fitness and to climbing Carrauntoohil. It starts with just 20 minutes walking per day. I'm
feeling pretty pathetic that that's where I'm at, but I do it anyway.
My wonderful husband and our twin boys agree to train with me
on the local hills. We commit to a Sunday morning walk, building
it up each week over Lent, until we celebrate on Easter Sunday
morning re-doing that 12k hike that had first sent me to get help.

I manage it with relative ease this time. I keep seeing my physiotherapist and I keep my three men in my support camp as we
start to do more ambitious mountain climbs in preparation for
Carrauntoohil in June. I'm feeling proud and I'm definitely fitter.
But I am also very conscious of an internal nagging voice: "This
isn't much fun, is it?" "Seriously, this is how you want to spend your
Sundays, trying to keep up with Andrew and the boys? You just
hold them back." On and on it goes, making me doubt if it is really
possible at all. I try to dial it down and persevere.

The day comes, two weeks before our big climb and we're on
the Galtee Mountains. We are each looking at the summit before
us and we're all thinking the same thing! "What are we doing out
here?" And: "Is Mum up to it?"

I have my head down, trundling along, grumpy because it isn't
easier and my boys are detecting weakness. They see an opportunity to bail out early and get home in time for the Saturday
afternoon sports show . . . "You know Mom, if we turn back now,
we'd be back in the car in an hour!" "We could get the fire lighting,
Mom, and you could just relax for the rest of today." Man, am I
tempted! And in truth, the boys are just saying what I'm thinking.

I look up at the ridge. It feels like it's still the same distance
away as when we started, even though we've been walking for over
an hour. I am so tempted to turn back. That internal, dissuading

voice is at it too: "Why not pack it in?" "Try again another day!" "I think Andrew has us on the wrong route anyway," like it's his fault that I'm tempted to jack it in.

And I recognize these thought patterns. They've been here throughout this whole journey of preparation for Carrauntoohil, doubting, dissuading, undermining my commitment. I have a flash of insight that if I give up now, I'll never do it. Everything hangs on the precipice. I realize I've had to make so many decisions in support of this dream: to get help from a physiotherapist, to get my husband and kids on board, to allow them to support me, to get up every Sunday no matter what and do that day's climb. And now I have another decision to make: to press on or go back?

You already know the decision I make! I press on. I tell the boys in no uncertain terms that I need them to stop suggesting quitting. It is as much as I can do to fight my inner voice of dis-couragement; I can't fight theirs too! Being the decent souls that they are, they comply. And instead, they encourage me. "You can do it, Mom." "You've got this, Mom." And with every step I take, I'm repeating my mantra, "It's my dream to do this. I've got what it takes. I don't have to enjoy it all the time, I just need to commit."

We walk and walk for hours. We get lost. I sit on my butt to literally slide down one steep slope, because in truth I have no energy to walk it. What should have been a 3–4 hour climb takes 6 and a bit. I'm shattered.

But I also know that I have summitted Carrauntoohil today on the Galtees! I wrestled with my internal voice of dissuasion and I won. Two weeks later I do it in situ. A proud mom, with her husband, twin boys, and her brother as their guide, conquers Carrauntoohil and makes it down in one piece!

People tell you that the way to climb a mountain is one step at a time. But I know a different reality. The way to climb a mountain is by climbing the slope of your thoughts. It's over a year later when my mentor shares with me that idea from Nelson Mandela. He spoke of how during his 27 years in prison, he had to overcome the internal negative self-talk, time and time and time again. He had to climb the slope of his thoughts. I have to do that too, consistently reaching for a more empowering thought. That's how I climbed Ireland's highest mountain. The memory of that lesson serves me with every goal I achieve. You have to climb the slope of your thoughts, every time, to achieve new heights in life and love.

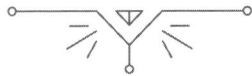

This or Something Better

Sherri Jaye
CALIFORNIA, USA

"How am I going to meet the man of my dreams if we don't go out in the evenings?" I pose this question to my friend on the fourth night of our seven-day cruise. We dress and decide to roam the ship to see some nightlife. Stumbling upon the piano bar, I hear show tunes. In we stroll and find the two seats left at the piano area. We're given a sheet of paper with a list of popular show tunes, and the first song that shouts out to me is "Some Enchanted Evening" from *South Pacific*. I tell the pianist I would like to hear him play it. Looking over to my right, I notice a gentleman, very dashing and charming, wearing a hat. He looks right at me and sings in a deep baritone voice with an interesting accent. (Just my luck, I think, he's probably from Austria or some place far away.) Unmistakably, he is singing just to me, "Some enchanted evening, you may see a stranger across a crowded room . . ." How did I not know those were the lyrics after all these years of hearing it? We both sing the song, he looking right at me, and suddenly I feel very coy and shy. I look down, I look at him, I look away. Is he flirting with me? My stomach is fluttering, my heart beats faster, I turn red and feel hot inside. Oh my goodness, what if he is "The One?"

After almost ten years of studying, becoming a life coach, and teaching others how to manifest a life they would love, I am ready to meet *him* on this cruise. I hear him tell the piano man to play "Matchmaker, Matchmaker," from *Fiddler on the Roof*, a mirror of my family's story and one of my favorite songs. How did he know? We sing to each other all night, and let me tell you, it was my enchanted evening. On the other side of me, witnessing this magic, sits my friend, all knowing. It is closing time at the piano bar; we look at one another and say goodnight.

I can't sleep, I feel the excitement over what might lie ahead, the possibilities and how cool it is to attract a man on this "Law of Attraction" cruise.

The next day is a blur, but I feel full of hope that he will be at the cocktail party the following evening. At the party I sit, all dolled up, drinking champagne when I see him. I wonder if he is part of this group. I walk right over to him and ask. He doesn't know what "group" I am talking about, so I explain to him the Law of Attraction and Esther Hicks.

He is interested and says he always believed in this philosophy. We exchange names and I ask him where he is from, as I couldn't place his accent. He says he was born in Mexico and now lives in Laguna Niguel. Not too far from me, phew! I had spoken to a lovely couple at dinner about this man I met in the piano bar the night before. They walk by while we are chatting and I introduce him to them. The woman says to him (his name is Sal, short for Salvador), "Did you get her phone number and address yet?" He says no, and immediately takes his iPad out and asks me for my information. We agree to meet in the piano bar later that night and he leaves for his dinner with his cousin. I just can't believe this is happening. But it is! I knew it, but when it's happening, it's like a dream or a movie. Later that night we all go to the piano bar. He walks in and it's like, oh my goodness, this isn't a dream. We spend the night singing, drinking, and just enjoying each other and the music. Finally, the piano bar closes, my friends leave us, and we are alone together for the first time.

We decide to find another place to continue our meeting. We spend the night sharing stories about ourselves. With pride, resiliency, and confidence, I tell him about my journey and how I haven't dated in almost 10 years. That I am looking to be in a relationship with a man who is emotionally available, stable, loving, and so much more. I explain that I am a life coach and that I have been helping people to live a life they would love. He is very interested in me and my life. He then shares with me about his life up until now. We are excited about the possibilities we have and realize this is such a great opportunity we have right here and now.

Do we dive in? Do we take the chance? We are together the next few days, which are heavenly and very dreamlike. He is flying to see his daughters for the 4th of July weekend. I am going home to have my annual 4th of July party where I am on cloud nine talking about him to my friends and family who cannot believe I have found "Him."

We text and speak on the phone for the next week until he comes to my house for our first date! He is so romantic and brings me flowers, takes me to a lovely place for dinner and then to Beverly Hills to a famous piano bar. The perfect first date.

We just celebrated eleven wonderful years together. We are retired now, live in Baja, Mexico with our three delightful puppies on a gorgeous bluff in our beautiful casa we manifested. Not to mention the most spectacular and breathtaking sunsets and moon-sets I've ever seen. I celebrate my dream of having a loving soulmate become a reality and thanking the Universe for bringing this and so much better!

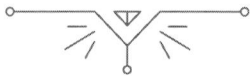

The Gift of Time

Heather D'Amore
MARYLAND, USA

I loved the feeling of crisp autumn air brushing across my cheeks.

Gazing skyward, the golden slides of sunbeams streaming towards the horizon reminded me of the playgrounds of my youth, especially the slides.

During that innocent time in my life, I thought these kind of ground-touching sunbeams were the angels' playground slides because, of course, angels needed to have fun too!

I remembered an afternoon at the playground with my mom, looking at how beautiful the sky was, a sky just like this one. Hugging me close to her side, she whispered in her magical voice, "When beams of sunshine stream to the ground they are Heaven's Golden Pathways reaching down to Earth to gather up loved ones that are ready to travel Home to Heaven to live amongst the angels."

"Mommy," I tearfully said, as I took her hand, holding on as tightly as I could, "I don't want to go to Heaven. I already have a home and you are my angel!" She smiled and kissed me on the cheek, and off we went to play on the slide.

It felt so wonderful to be brought back to such a sweet moment in time, after all these years.

"Heather, it's time." Leaving those memories and the beauty of the sky behind, I went inside to join my family. After greeting everyone I walked over to check on a very special loved one, resting in another room. Quietly, I opened the door, and a feeling of serenity washed over me, as I watched the sweet face of one that I love resting so peacefully there.

At that moment time seemed to change—no longer feeling linear—as years of treasured memories came and went, from one to the other, in no special sequence. They began to play out in my mind, like little video clips that I was in, while another part of me seemed to be watching from outside the frame.

My family gathered around a New Year's Eve campfire outside the mountaintop home of dear friends in Vermont. Glowing firelight flickered across their peaceful faces as they dreamed up New Year's Resolutions to be shared with all at the stroke of midnight.

I'm camped on an island with my family, tiptoeing into our old canvas tent hoping not to wake my sisters and brother as I notice their peacefully sleeping faces and wonder what they are dreaming about.

I am nine years old, and quite the tomboy. While playing outside by the stream, I find a tiny baby turtle by the water's edge. I scoop it up in the palm of my hand, and hurry home to show my mom. When I get there mom is taking her afternoon nap and looks so peaceful as she rests.

I tiptoed right up to her face holding my turtle two inches from her nose, so it will be the first thing she sees when I wake her up. "Mommy, wake up! I have a surprise for you."

She opens her eyes, sees the turtle, and screams, mouth wide open. Startled, I fall forward towards her face, causing my turtle to fall into her mouth. As she coughs, the turtle falls onto the covers, unharmed.

I can't stop laughing. Much to my surprise, my mom doesn't think it's funny at all. In fact, she slept with her arm over her mouth for all the years that followed.

Another memory of my mother comes back to me now. I hear her saying "Always be grateful for the gift of time, and value every minute, instead of wasting it on thoughts, feelings and actions that diminish your sense of aliveness. Be present, for tomorrow is not promised, and today is your *gift*. Always be kind and compassionate with yourself and especially to those in need." Oh, how I love remembering her voice and hearing her words of wisdom in my mind once again.

Called back to the present by the sound of a harmonica being played by my sister in the next room, I think of my brother, whose heartfelt harmonica playing inspired all who heard him. All the memories quickly take their place back in my mind, and I am once again aware of being in the room feeling a peaceful presence that wraps itself around me like a comforting warm blanket of love. I walk further into the room, where my dear brother rests. He looks so peaceful.

I remember the special feeling of holding him the day he was born.

My five-year-old self decided he was my baby, too. I told my mother that she would have to share him because I was going to be his mommy as well. She told me that was fine, as long as I shared in the Mommy chores, which meant changing his diapers. Thinking quickly, I replied "That's okay Mommy, I changed my mind, I think I will just be his sister instead." I asked if I could kiss his

244 ✧ THE GIFT OF TIME

cute baby cheeks, and she said, "Yes, as long as you don't wake him up, because he is resting so peacefully."

"Shawn," I whisper ever so softly, as I leaned down to quietly to give him a soft kiss on his cheek, "Just so you know, Bro, I will be looking for four leaf clovers, pennies on the ground, and for hummingbirds and cardinals that show up unexpectedly, and while I am at it, I will look for rainbows, and know it's you sending me 'signs' that you are with me."

I understand more fully now than ever before the value of time, and will be more grateful for the gift of time that I am given. In your honor, I will use my life as you did, being a beacon of love, light, laughter and compassion.

Thank you for loving me and always believing in me. I am so grateful to have experienced such a soulful connection as ours, and know it will continue throughout time.

It was time to leave my brother's side, I held his hand and kissed him on the cheek one last time. I whispered softly, reminding him to send me lots of signs, and told him I loved him.

As I went outside, I looked up and saw the setting sun with the golden pathways of light ascending into heaven, and I knew my brother was going home to be with the angels and that he would be our angel forever more.

Featured Contributors

Aurelie Cormier

Aurelie Cormier is a proud mom, and an Oncology/Women's Health Nurse Practitioner who values education, creativity, and making a difference. Her focus is Prevention, Survivorship and Healing; it is her life's passion. There are steps. She knows our genes are not our destiny, and sometimes our greatest struggles lead to our greatest achievements; that has been true for her life.

She worked in the trenches for 41 years, dedicated to helping her patients regain their health, most having complex cancers, lymphomas, and multiple myelomas. She witnessed their suffering, financial struggles, and helped with their treatments, complications, recurrences, remissions, cures and end-of-life moments. She loves to help families envision and create their dreams, focused on Abundant Health and Wellbeing!

Benjamin Blackett

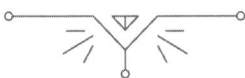

Benjamin Blackett has been featured on CBS News, ABC, NBC, and FOX with his Transformational Life Coaching Business, A Creative Healing Place.

Benjamin's personal transformational journey winds through a variety of paths, including framing houses, painting houses, and restoring historical buildings; working in professional theatre as an actor, master electrician, stage manager, and director; living in France; becoming a Middle School French teacher; driving boats for pleasure and work; becoming a TranscenDance™ Facilitator; and finally to leading transformational retreats in the South of France in which he combines teaching, Stand Up Paddling in the Mediterranean Sea, and exposing his clients to amazing French culture and cuisine.

Benjamin is a great leader, teacher and an amazing adventurer.

Cheetra Ramcharn

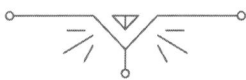

Cheetra Ramcharn is a coach and energy healer. She grew up in Mauritius and currently resides in Toronto, Canada.

She has a Degree in Systems Analysis and Design (British Computer Society). She is a Life Mastery Consultant, certified with the Brave Thinking Institute. She is a Law of Attraction Coach, certified with the Quantum Success Coaching Academy. She is a Reiki Master.

For over 20 years, Cheetra has been studying and implementing transformational success principles. As a coach, she helps her clients to discover and fully live their life's purpose! She uses visualization, law of attraction and energy shifting processes to empower her clients to take responsibility for their life and to bring forth the solutions from their own infinite wisdom.

A Reiki master, she intuitively helps release energy blocks within the body, the free flow of energy then allows healing to occur naturally.

Cynthia D. Lamberth

Cynthia D. Lamberth, PhDc, MPH, CLMC is an internationally known Leadership Strategist, Author, and Coach. Cynthia is passionate about serving others, equipping and empowering them to design and live a life they love to serve their purpose, community, family, friends, tribe, and world.

For over 35 years, she and her team have developed and delivered leadership programs, workshops, and coaching sessions for corporations, governmental organizations, universities, and associations. Now through ExudeU, this time-tested wisdom is available to individuals and organizations. She and her husband live in Babcock Ranch, Florida, in the home their dreams built.

She is a lifelong learner and achiever, has published extensively, completed numerous half-marathons, is a successful entrepreneur, and, most importantly, a wife, mom, and gran.

Dawn Zehren

Dawn Zehren is a coach, speaker and life strategist. Her purpose is to help people end the pain of pretending to be less than they truly are so that they manifest their dreams. Clients realize harmonious families, red-hot romance, vibrant health, adventure, business success and more.

Dawn's passions include sharing stories and meals, creating crafts and events, and laughing out loud. When traveling you'll find her checking out used bookstores, historical sites, and rock shops. She lives in beautiful Wauwatosa (Milwaukee), Wisconsin with her talented husband Nick, and their magnificent dog, Jack.

Are you ready to begin manifesting your dreams? Take advantage of Dawn's free tools at www.DawnZehren.com.

Donald Brunnert

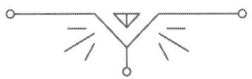

Donald Brunnert is a Life Coach, Program Leader, and author. His unique focus is on building skills that transform individuals' strengths and confidence into unlimited resources to reach their most elusive personal and professional goals.

Donald has studied under the mentorship of leading figures in the personal and professional growth field—a journey that led him to becoming a certified life coach specializing in mindset coaching. With his husband, Jason, Donald co-founded Team Affect Consultant: a personal, professional, and leadership development company. He loves watching clients build the lives of their dreams as they realize and tap into the potential that dwells within them.

Donusia Lipinski

Donusia Lipinski's journey of self-care and healing culminated in becoming a Life Mastery Consultant and a High-Performance Coach. When multiple tragedies occurred in 2004, Donusia knew her path to recovery would take her on a profound transformative spiritual quest.

Donusia served immigrants and businesses as a heart-centered immigration lawyer for over 37 years before certification as a Life Coach. Today she uses that experience to empower legal professionals who feel stuck, stressed, and overwhelmed to design lives they love living. She is the founder of Grace and Ease Life Coaching, LLC.

Donusia earned her Juris Doctorate from Golden Gate University in San Francisco. Before becoming a lawyer, Donusia was an elementary education teacher and an autoworker for Ford Motor Company.

Hanna Gorecka

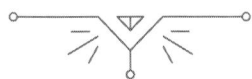

Hanna Gorecka is a certified Dream Builder Coach with a BA in Psychology. She is a successful entrepreneur and has years of leadership experience in Human Resources.

Faced with devastating life circumstance, Hanna had a choice, to live in a reclusive survival mode or to take steps to rebuild a meaningful life. She chose to focus on healing. In the process, Hanna also discovered her desire to help people heal and rebuild their life after a challenging event. Her work is dedicated primarily to helping women cultivate their deeper sense of self love and fostering the importance of connection to the community.

You can discover more about Hanna at www.findmyway.ca.

Heather D'Amore

In the beginning there was my mom, my first spiritual teacher. She was intuitive, creative, inspiring and taught me that the key to a meaningful life was to decide in advance to learn something valuable from every situation, no matter how challenging, by activating empowered thinking and faith.

My desire to learn about spirituality took root and started to grow at an early age as a result. I have since studied with many renowned teachers, including Mary M. Morrissey, Bears and Samahria Kaufman from the Option Institute, Joe Dispenza, and Bruce H. Lipton.

I am a certified Life Mastery Consultant, DreamBuilder Coach, Option Process Mentor, Vision Board Workshop Facilitator, and have trained and worked at the A.R.E./Edgar Cayce Foundation in the Healing Arts.

I offer dynamic interactive Dream Builder/VisionBoard workshops, group and individual coaching programs. I am here to help! Heather@damoreuknow.com

Jason Brumfield

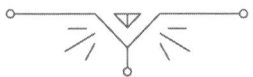

Jason Brumfield is an educator, life coach, and author. He has enjoyed a 20+ year career in education that started in a suburban New Orleans high school classroom as an English teacher. He currently serves as the Secondary Reading Language Arts Coordinator for a school district in North Texas.

Jason has studied under the mentorship of leading figures in the personal and professional growth field—a journey that led him to becoming a certified life coach specializing in mindset coaching. With his husband, Donald, Jason co-founded Team Affect Consultant: a personal, professional, and leadership development company. He loves watching clients build the lives of their dreams as they realize and tap into the potential that dwells within them.

Joan Luke

Joan Luke has walked the path of brave thinking many times since her childhood in the valley of Los Angeles to become a top results leader. Drawing on her years of study, she empowers successful women to craft their Soul-inspired vision. Joan is an inspirational speaker, author, and Certified Life Mastery coach. The interactive vision workshops she delivers on stages and on Zooms awaken and ignite the power within others to be more than they thought possible, up until now.

Joan delights in her clients' successes and feels blessed to support individuals and groups to transform and live their dream lives now!

Joan lives with her childhood crush, Lawrence, in San Clemente, California.

Discover more and connect today at www.JoanLuke.com.

Linda Lee Smith

Linda Lee Smith is a certified Dreambuilder Coach and Life Mastery consultant through the Brave Thinking® Institute, the premier coaching program on visioning a life you truly would love to live created by Mary Morrissey, Transformational Leader. Linda has a rich background that she brings to her clients, including certifications in Holistic Nursing, Energy Healing (Healing Touch), and Clinical Aromatherapy. She is married to her husband coach, Rich Schmelke whom she met and fell in love with at the age of 70. Together they promote Transformational Wellness through their coaching to individuals, couples, and groups.

Lisa Phelan

Lisa is a spiritually-based certified Life, Health and Business coach and speaker. She works with both men and women to achieve a whole wealth life. Lisa knows she is just a guide for her clients, holding them with love and showing them they can truly live a life they love. She knows people are more powerful and contain more potential than any circumstance, situation, or condition.

When she's not running her business, you will find Lisa helping animals. Lisa lives with her partner Ed and two dogs, Jake and Rollo. She has two adult children, two bonus kids and four grandchildren. Her favorite things are God, family/friends, her clients and tennis. She splits her time between the Bahamas and New Hampshire.

Margie Ziegler

Margie Ziegler is the founder of Dream Life Ignited LLC, a Life Mastery Consultant, and a healing arts practitioner on a mission to inspire women to live vibrantly with freedom and impact.

She uses her diverse skills to connect with the core of one's authentic being and to evoke the best in each individual.

She has supported the Chopra Center, the Brave Thinking Institute, Ozaukee Women's Network, and Toastmasters International as a volunteer.

She won first place at a Toastmasters speaking contest.

Margie was a guest speaker at the Superconscious Success Summit, an international online event featuring coaches and healers.

Some of her passions are nature, travel, visiting her granddaughters, and hiking trails with her Golden Retriever.

Mary K. Ott

Mary K. Ott is a sought-after International Transformational Coach, professional speaker, and author. Having multiple certifications including Certified Life Mastery Consultant, and Certified Jack Canfield Trainer, she has collectively helped hundreds of clients to overcome limitations, dissolve fears, create clarity, and build their dreams.

Her personal transformational journey began at age sixteen with a book that changed her life forever. She enjoys continuous, ongoing personal learning, reading, writing, painting, traveling the globe, and entertaining family and friends. She lives in rural New Jersey with her husband of 33 years and two cats.

Pat Acklie-Roth

Pat Acklie-Roth, of Life Changing Coaching & Consulting, has served others for 56 years: Transformational Life Coach, Life Mastery Consultant, author, and Grief Recovery Specialist. Summers, she's in her sewing studio in the northeast and coaching. Winters, she's in Texas coaching full-time.

Coaching ended a 30-year marriage, designed a new life and found her the love of her life.

She teaches others how to go from where they are to where they want to be and change their results.

Pat studied with Mary Morrissey at Brave Thinking Institute and Bob Proctor at Proctor Gallagher Institute, constantly learning.

She lost her son, mother, brother, and husband. After going through grief counseling, she contacted the Grief Recovery Institute and became a Licensed Grief Recovery Specialist.

Richard (Rich) Schmelke

Richard (Rich) Schmelke is a certified Dreambuilder coach and Life Mastery consultant through the Brave Thinking Institute, the premier coaching program on visioning a life you truly love living, created by Mary Morrissey, Transformational Leader. Rich is also certified as a Clinical Aromatherapy Practitioner.

Rich has practiced one form or another of personal development for over 40 years. He is married to the love of his life and fellow transformational life coach, Linda Lee Smith, whom he met and fell in love with at the age of 69.

Rich and Linda promote Transformational Wellness through their coaching of individuals, couples, and groups.

Sharon Tala

For 25 years, Sharon Tala has helped people of all ages navigate life's challenges in a safe, loving space. With her diverse holistic training and keen intuition, she guides others through break-throughs they never thought were possible.

She uses her unique skills and proven methodologies to help people experience harmony and balance within their body, mind and spirit. Her passion is to see others transform into who they truly are, not who they or others think they should be. Sharon meets you where you are, coaching and cheering you on with unconditional love and acceptance so you can experience peace and vitality in every area of your life.

Sigrid Igland

Sigrid Igland is a coach, speaker, and mother, whose mission is to empower teenagers and their families. Back in school, Sigrid used to be so afraid of the teachers that she would over-prepare, get nervous, and not really learn. Then she discovered the power of having a clear vision of what she wanted from school.

Since then, studying, getting good grades, and enjoying life became playful and fun. And she promised herself that if she made it through school, she would help the ones coming after. Now, having reaped the benefits of her vision, and with years of training with global experts, she helps students build their vision, so they go from striving to thriving in their school years and beyond.

Theresa Garvin

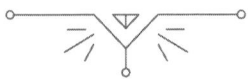

Theresa Garvin is an LICSW and a transformational coach. She has been providing psychotherapy and counseling services to children, teens, families, and adults for over 35 years. Theresa has focused much of her work in supporting those who are diagnosed with ADHD, anxiety, depression, and other childhood disorders. She has also been an Adjunct Professor at Boston College, Graduate School of Social Work.

After her own study of transformational laws and principles in 2017, Theresa became certified as a Life Mastery Consultant through the Brave Thinking Institute. She is now the owner and founder of The Life You Imagine, where she helps individuals and families to find their focus, to thrive, and to create lives they absolutely love living.

Trish Walker

Trish Walker is an intuitive coach, healer, speaker and movie producer who lives in the Utah mountains. She previously worked in the medical device industry and now coaches others through major life milestones, whether it be a new decade, divorce, job loss or grief.

Through her journey, she has been certified in several healing and coaching modalities. Trish has recently signed on as Executive Producer for a short film which is fueling her passion for the film and TV industry. A mom of one, Trish is on a journey of self-discovery, role modeling and joy as her son gets ready to leave the nest. Trish's book, *Oh Honey I'm Just Getting Started!*, can be found on Amazon and on her website at www.trishwalker.us.

Made in the USA
Monee, IL
23 July 2023

39611916R00153